Veloce *Classic Reprint* Series

THE HALF-TON

# MILITARY LAND ROVER

- MARK J. COOK -

I0808628

First published in 2001 and reprinted in 2004 and August 2010, this Veloce Classic Reprint published June 2019 by Veloce Publishing Limited, Veloce House, Parkway Farm Business Park, Middle Farm Way, Poundbury, Dorchester, Dorset, DT1 3AR, England. Fax 01305 250479/Tel 01305 260068/e-mail info@veloce.co.uk/web www.veloce.co.uk or www.velocebooks.com.
ISBN: 978-1-787115-45-3 UPC: 6-36847-01545-9



Readers with ideas for automotive books, or books on other transport or related hobby subjects, are invited to write to the editorial director of Veloce Publishing at the above address.
British Library Cataloguing in Publication Data – A catalogue record for this book is available from the British Library. Typesetting, design and page make-up all by Veloce Publishing Ltd on Apple Mac.
Printed and bound by CPI Group (UK) Ltd, Croydon, CR0 4YY.


Front cover image courtesy of Clive Elliott. Military Police Series 3 FFR Hard Top at Bovington Camp in 1994

Veloce *Classic Reprint* Series

# THE HALF-TON MILITARY LAND ROVER

- MARK J. COOK -

VELOCE PUBLISHING
THE PUBLISHER OF FINE AUTOMOTIVE BOOKS

# CONTENTS

# GLOSSARY OF ACRONYMS

| | |
|---|---|
| AATDC | Army Air Transport Training and Development Centre. |
| AC | Army Code. |
| ACP | Automatic Colt Pistol. |
| APGP | Air Portable General Purpose, 109" Land Rover based on Rover 9. |
| APV | Armoured Patrol Vehicle, Glover Webb conversion of LR 110, and Defender 110. |
| ATTRUM | Amphibious Trials and Training Unit Royal Marines. |
| BAT | Battalion Anti-Tank gun, (British 120mm recoilless series). |
| BATUS | British Army Training Unit Suffield (Canada). |
| BCF | Bromochlorodifluoromethane (Halon 1211). |
| CAV | Courtaulds Armoured Vehicle, based on Defender 110, with composite plastic armour, often called Snatch. |
| CKD | Completely Knocked Down, Land Rover in unassembled pack. |
| CL | Military term for Commercial Logistic (Land Rover commercial model, with minimum modifications for military use). |
| EMER | Electrical and Mechanical Engineering Regulations, REME, support publications. |
| EOD | Explosive Ordnance Disposal. |
| FACE | Field Artillery Computer Equipment. |
| FFR | Fitted For Radio, standardised basic provision in vehicle, to fit, without further modification, Larkspur, and later (or if modified), Clansman radio system sets. |
| FVRDE | Fighting Vehicles Research and Development Establishment. Merged with MEXE to become MVEE on 1 April 1970. |
| GPMG | General Purpose Machine Gun, 7.62mm, British version of Belgian FN MAG. |
| GRP | Glass Reinforced Plastic (armour). |
| GS | General Service. |
| HMMWV | High Mobility Multi-purpose Wheeled Vehicle. |
| IED | Improvised Explosive Device. |
| IRR | Infra Red Reflective. |
| JATE | Joint Air Trials Establishment. |
| MCE | Marshall of Cambridge Engineering Ltd. |
| MEXE | Military Engineering Experimental Establishment. |
| mil | Military measurement of degrees (6400 mils = 360 degrees). |
| MoD | Ministry of Defence. |
| MSP | Medium Stressed Platform, used for parachute dropping of various permutations of vehicles, artillery, etc. Impact is reduced by the use of air bags. |
| MVEE | Military Vehicles and Engineering Establishment. |

| | |
|---|---|
| NATO | North Atlantic Treaty Organisation. |
| ORBAT | Order of Battle. |
| PADS | Position and Azimuth Determining System, navigational system made by Ferranti. |
| POL | Petrol, oil, lubricants. |
| REME | Royal Electrical Mechanical Engineers. |
| RUC | Royal Ulster Constabulary. |
| TA | Territorial Army. |
| TAOR | Tactical Area of Responsibility. |
| TOW | Tube-launched Optically tracked Wire-guided, a heavy wire-guided anti-tank missile system. |
| UDR | Ulster Defence Regiment. |
| VPK | Vehicle Protection Kit. (see Northern Ireland). |
| WD | War Department. |
| XPM | Expanded plate metal mesh. |
| 7.62mm | Calibre in millimetres of NATO standard ammunition. |

– For Mum and Dad –

# INTRODUCTION & THANKS

I decided to write this book after speaking to a fellow enthusiast who was looking for information about the M40 A1 recoilless rifle Lightweights. It occurred to me that no one had actually written a book about the Land Rover Lightweight, even though they are among the most popular of the Land Rovers. If I had known in the beginning how much work would be involved, of course, it's possible I might not have begun this book at all ...

Although much of what is written in these pages may be common knowledge amongst military Land Rover enthusiasts, much has come to light during the course of my research which has not been published before. One thing which has become very clear is that there is no such thing as a standard Half-Ton Land Rover, even when considering only one model, such is the versatility of the vehicle.

I am greatly indebted to all those who helped me in my research, without which this book would have lacked much of its substance. I am particularly indebted to the following:

Philip Bashall of The Dunsfold Land Rover Collection, for letting me search for and borrow material from the archive. Philip Chatfield; Andy Cross of Marshall Military Engineering; John Delaney of the Imperial War Museum's photo archives department; David Eason; Clive Elliott; Mark Finch; Tom Finlay; Peter Jarman of The Road Transport Fleet Data Society; Steve Marsh; John Mastrangelo; Eric Pagan; Martin Pagh; Guy Pelham; Nick Percival; Ron Prestleton; and, especially, Bob Seager. I would also like to thank the Royal Electrical and Mechanical Engineers' Museum of Technology at Arborfield, The Royal Logistic Corps Museum, The Royal Marines Museum, and The Sectie Militaire Geschiedenis of the Royal Netherlands Army, all of which kindly contributed photographs.

I hope that this book will be of interest to military vehicle enthusiasts and, in particular, to anyone restoring a Lightweight to its military specification. I hope also that it will prove to have equal appeal to model makers, and to Land Rover enthusiasts in general.

Note: Whilst the Land Rover Half-Ton is now often referred to as the 'Lightweight,' this was not the case in military circles or at Land Rover, so within the book the Lightweight is generally referred to as the 'Half-Ton.'

**Mark J Cook**

***Bessbrook Mill 1983. (Courtesy Royal Marines Museum)***

# 1

# ROVER 1

## Introduction to the Military Land Rover

After the Second World War, the Rover Car Company, then based at Solihull, near Birmingham, found that it had a major problem in that the amount of steel it was allocated was limited (due to post-war shortages and because of rationing). Although Rover was well known at that time for its cars, there was very little public demand for them in the austerity years after the war. The only cars available were pre-war models since no development work on new models was undertaken during the war (all production and engineering having been concentrated on the war effort). An additional problem was that the Government rationed cars for the home market, and encouraged motor vehicle manufacturers to export. Priority was given to exporters that could bring in much needed revenue to help Britain's war ravaged economy.

Because there was no demand for Rover cars (and very little steel), Maurice Wilks, Rover's chief designer, came up with the idea of developing a new vehicle (to be called the Land Rover) to replace the war surplus Jeeps used by many farmers. The design would use an aluminium body on a steel box-frame chassis (aluminium was plentiful at the time since it was not subject to rationing). In the end it was decided to work with Birmabright aluminium alloy, even though it was much more expensive than sheet steel. This material also had excellent corrosion resistance, a commendable thing in an agricultural machine.

Between March and May 1948, the

***Austin Champ on a Medium Stressed Platform. The Champ was to be replaced by the Land Rover. (Courtesy John Mastrangelo)***

***The Austin Gipsy was assessed in trials for possible military use in the early 1960s. This is a 3/4 Ton version. (Courtesy Ken Porter)***

first 48 pre-production Land Rovers were made, and at least two of these went to the Ministry of Supply for testing. The outcome of these trials was that, in 1948, an initial order for 48 vehicles was placed for the British Army, and a second order for 1878 vehicles soon followed.

Ever since then the British Armed Services have used Land Rovers in huge numbers and in a wide variety of roles. Many were based on largely civilian types, with only minor modifications for military use.

Land Rover conducted experiments with a variety of new vehicles over the years, most of these, however, fell by the wayside. Examples included the Truck 1 Ton 4x4 Airportable General Purpose in 1962, and the 3/4 Ton 4x4 Cargo (with a 6-cylinder engine) in 1966. It was during the 1960s, however, that Land Rover was asked by the War Department (WD) to submit a design for a new lightweight airportable vehicle. This was, after much work, to become one of the most successful of the military Land Rovers ever built, with very large numbers used by all three British Armed Services, and by a great many foreign forces too. Its many roles would include general transport and cargo, emergency ambulance, recoilless rifle carrier, radar carrier, reconnaissance, internal security, bomb disposal, command post/communications and line laying, and it would see service in several conflicts.

For a vehicle that was intended as a stopgap (until sheet steel became available again), the Land Rover was an amazing success, not only in the military, but also in civilian life. The Lightweight, or Half-Ton as it was more usually referred to, has proved to be most successful within the British

***Opposite top: 89 AA 73 is an RAF Rover 8 GS, large numbers of which were built from 1961 to 1966. (Courtesy Ken Porter)***

***Opposite bottom: 10 ER 94 is a Rover 8 FFR, large numbers of which were also built from 1961 to 1966, after which the Rover 10 was introduced. No Rover 10 FFR vehicles were built since the Rover 1 FFR was used for the role. (Courtesy Ken Porter)***

V/38
89 AA 73

49
10 ER 94

22FG78

SPORTS FIELD
CHANGING ROOM
42AM48

Armed Services of course, with no serious contenders within its load class (it was never intended to be available new on the civilian market).

Abroad, other versions of the Half-Ton were made by the Spanish, and later, the Iranians (see Chapter 5).

This is the story of the Lightweight.

## Background to the Rover 1

In the early 1960s, the average helicopter could not lift any significant weight, nor any of the 1/4 ton vehicles available at the time. In a drive to come up with a more airportable vehicle, the US Marine Corps came up with the 'Mighty Mite', which was manufactured by American Motors from April 1960 to January 1963. The Mid America Research Corporation actually started development of this vehicle in 1950, from a design by Ben F. Gregory, and the US Marine Corps tested twelve prototypes in the early 1950s. The wheelbase was only 64in and the vehicle weighed 1496lb (678kg). The engine was air-cooled, and transmission was via a 3 speed high/low range gearbox and permanent 4x4.

American Motors Corporation began to manufacture this vehicle in November 1954, but it still took 6 years to start quantity production. By the time production stopped, about 3922 vehicles had been delivered to the US Marine Corp.

Known as the 'Truck 1/4 Ton 4x4 Utility Lightweight M422 and M422 A1' (the letter denoting a modified version), the production model differed in many respects from the prototypes. The production model featured a 4 speed gearbox, 4x4 could be disengaged, the engine was a V4 instead of inline (though it was still air-cooled), the wheelbase was now 71in, and the vehicle now weighed 1700lb. This was a good early example of a successful airportable military vehicle.

Airportable vehicles became somewhat fashionable in the early 1960s, with various countries experimenting with lightweight vehicles of one type or another.

Although Britain still had interests in various parts of the world at the time, the Army, and its many foreign garrisons, was shrinking. This meant that the Armed Forces needed to be able to get equipment and men quickly to destinations abroad. Amphibious and airborne formations, therefore, became very important.

The War Department also wanted a lightweight 4x4, and began testing the existing 1/4 Ton (the FV1801 Austin Champ), minus the body, by parachuting them on pallets from aircraft. The end results, however, were often disastrous as vehicles were often damaged and often landed in the wrong place. Vehicles were tested by the Fighting Vehicles Research and Development Establishment (FVRDE), which had extensive test facilities at sites at Chertsey, Chobham, Bagshot Heath and Long Valley, amongst others. Other vehicles tested included the Hunting Harrier and the 2-cylinder Austrian Steyr-Puch Haflinger.

During 1959/1960, BMC introduced the Mini Moke, which incorporated some commercial components. It was among the first British attempts at developing an air-transportable military vehicle, being designed to be stacked 3 high using the mudguards! The original Moke was 4x2, with a 4x4 version being produced for evaluation in 1962. The War Department tested some but found that the Moke was not really suitable, one major problem being the lack of ground clearance.

During 1966 the Austin Ant 4x4 was produced to tempt the Ministry of Defence (MoD), as the War Department had become in 1962. However, in 1968 Austin was incorporated into British Leyland and, since the latter already had a 4x4 with the Land Rover, this effectively killed off the Austin Ant and the Gypsy. The civilian Austin Gipsy, which had been introduced in 1958, had also been tested for military use but, although it had a low weight, it was due to cease production in mid 1968.

***Opposite top: 22 FG 78 is a 1969 Rover 10 Station Wagon. The Rover 10 was effectively superseded by the Rover 1 Half Ton, but some special versions, such as the Station Wagon and Rover 10 CL, appeared in relatively small numbers. Note the civilian type lights. (Courtesy Ken Porter)***

***Opposite bottom: 42 AM 48 is a late RAF Rover 10 GS, with military chassis and lights. (Courtesy Ken Porter)***

The MoD was not truly happy with any of these designs, however, as they did not fully meet its requirements. In some desperation, the MoD asked Land Rover to have a look at the concept. By this time, the 88in wheelbase Land Rover remained the only vehicle in its class left in production.

The standard military 1/4 Ton (88in wheelbase) at this time was the Series IIA (see Appendix 1 for a complete listing of the Military Land Rover types), which had been introduced in 1961 (it was officially referred to as the 'Truck 4x4 GS (General Service) and FFR (Fitted For Radio) 1/4 Ton Rover 8'). In 1967, however, the Series IIA had been improved, with the introduction of negative earth and a number of other minor changes, and became the 'Truck 4x4 1/4 Ton GS Rover 10'. All three British Services used the Rover 8 and 10. Most of these had the then standard 2286cc petrol engine, slightly modified for military use (a small number, however, had diesel engines). The modifications for military use included a different water pump, fan, oil pump, timing cover and oil cooler. The 24 volt vehicles had a completely different electrical system.

From 1961 to 1967, a very large number of Rover 8 12 volt GS and 24 volt FFR vehicles were ordered and delivered. Only relatively small numbers of Rover 10 GS and 24 volt (but not FFR) vehicles were delivered, however, because the Rover 1 was to take its place, although this was not the original intention since only 75 Rover 1s were initially required. Confusingly, there were also the Rover 8 and 10 'Car Utility 1/4 Ton 4x4' (Station Wagon) models and the 'Truck CL 1/4 Ton' (Commercial Logistic) models.

Land Rover had tried a number of experiments with airportable vehicles in the past, notably with the 'Truck 1 Ton Airportable General Purpose (APGP) 4x4' based on a Series IIA 109in chassis. There were at least 20 of these built under contract WV579 in 1962-4. They carried the military registration numbers 16 EK 01 to 16 EK 20, and a number of them still survive. Incidentally, these vehicles were designed to float across rivers (being equipped with flotation kits), and they were also designed to be stacked upon each other for airportability. All were 24 volt FFR.

## The Early Years, Setting the Scene

Like everyone else at the time, the Royal Marines were also very eager to find a robust new vehicle which could be carried by the Royal Navy's newly improved Westland Wessex HU5 helicopters. These had come into service in 1964 as a specialist troop transport and load-carrying version of the Wessex, and were capable of carrying under-slung loads of roughly one and a half tons in average conditions.

Incidentally, on 6th November 1956, during the Suez Crisis, the Royal Marines had made the first British helicopter assault in history when they landed men at Port Said (using Sikorsky Whirlwinds).

*A Citroën 2CV underneath a Westland Wessex HAS 1. With the proposed introduction of the twin-engined Wessex HU5 in 1964, the search was on for a replacement for the 2CV. (Courtesy Royal Marines Museum)*

***The first prototype, in stripped down form, in October 1965. (Courtesy British Motoring Industry Heritage Trust)***

The prototype HU5 (Navy designation) flew on 31 May 1963, and 100, fitted with twin Rolls-Royce turbine Gnome engines, were delivered to the Royal Navy. The RAF also received 71 of these helicopters, though this time they were designated HC2.

From 1960 onwards, the Royal Marines used some 65 Citroën 2CV

*Another view of the first prototype, in its built up form. Of interest are the normal type door hinges (not flush), the flush type bonnet, outside bonnet catches and large military style bumper. (Courtesy Dunsfold Collection)*

*Publicity photograph of the first prototype. This shows the parts that could be removed to get the vehicle into the "Lightweight WD" form. Of note are the normal type door hinges (not flush), the door capping, no load area protection strips and no spare tyre mounting! (Courtesy Dunsfold Collection)*

pick-up trucks, minus the doors, airlifting them ashore using Westland Whirlwinds (HAS7s) flying off the converted carriers HMS Albion and HMS Bulwark. The Citroëns were selected principally because of their light weight, front wheel drive, and basic load carrying ability. The Citroëns' incredible suspension, however, meant that they could withstand repeated helicopter freight release landings from up to ten feet. It was intended that they would be the first vehicles ashore, carrying radio equipment, water, rations and ammunition.

The 2CV was chosen because, when stripped, it was light enough to be airlifted by the Whirlwinds. However, these vehicles were only to be a short term measure, for use until the introduction of the Wessex. They were also limited in that they could not carry any significant payload, and they were only 4x2. Despite their limitations, though, some actually saw service in Borneo during the Indonesian confrontation of 1963-66.

*The 3/4 Ton Airportable General Purpose was an early Land Rover attempt at an airportable vehicle. It was far too heavy for the Lightweight WD specification however.*
*(Courtesy John Mastrangelo)*

*Below: 20 BT 90 was an early prototype, seen here at a display sometime after 1970 since it displays the MVEE badge. Note the non-standard bonnet, which is less angled then normal. The bulkhead and hinges, steering wheel and axle drive flange ends, are different from the production vehicles. It was sold at Ruddington in October 1976.*
*(Courtesy Ken Porter)*

***Above: 20 BT 90 in its built up form. (Courtesy John Mastrangelo)***

The Army was also keen to have an airportable vehicle. In the early 1960s, the War Department issued a "General Staff requirement for a lightweight airportable helicopter-liftable vehicle that could carry a useful payload and be capable of towing light support weapons". The criterion for the maximum stripped-weight was that it could be lifted by the Wessex from sea level at Aden to the mountains inland at summer ambient temperatures (hence weights of 2500lb (1135kg) max). However, by the time it got into service, the Wessex had had a lot of extra equipment fitted, and couldn't

***The bulkhead top was removable, for clearance inside aircraft, as well as weight saving. This is a wooden fuselage mockup for a VC10. (Courtesy Airborne Forces Museum)***

21 BT 85
624 GC

624 GC
21 BT 85

21 BT 85

*Opposite: The Army Air Transport Training and Development Centre (AATDC), based at Old Sarum, Wiltshire, used the preproduction vehicles in airportability trials to establish and prove loading methods with various aircraft. In these views, vehicles are being trialed in a Lockheed C130 Hercules, borrowed from the USAF. The RAF at this time had ordered the C130 but was yet to receive any aircraft.*
*(Courtesy Airborne Forces Museum)*

*Above: A GS preproduction vehicle, in completely stripped down form. The preproduction vehicles were classed as $^1/_4$ Ton. (Courtesy Airborne Forces Museum)*

***Preproduction vehicle 21 BT 85 being put through its paces at the FVRDE Chertsey in September 1966. (Courtesy REME Museum)***

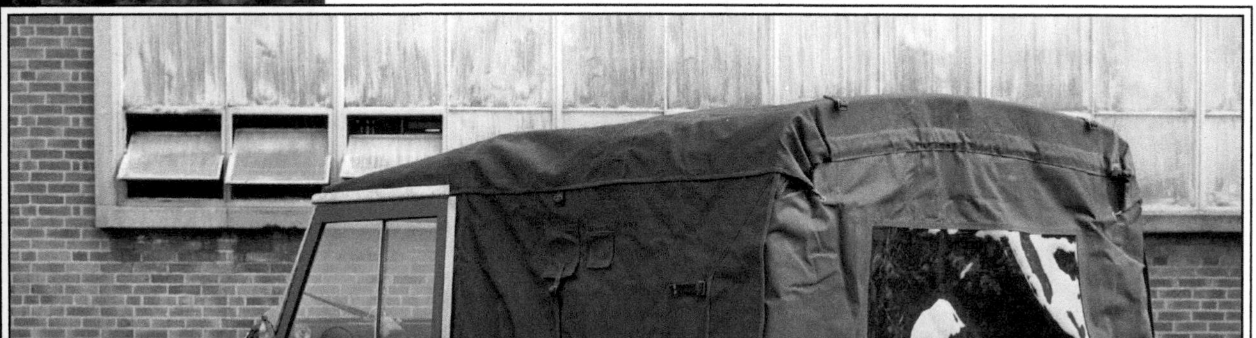

***Rear view of a preproduction GS vehicle in built up form, looking very much as a production vehicle. External minor detail differences include the mounting for the door mirrors, the door hinge design and recess shape, the numberplate mounting is square instead of oblong, the driving member ends are a slightly different design, there is no cut-out in the bonnet for the radio coaxial leads, and no toolbox fitted to the wheelarch. (Courtesy Dunsfold Collection)***

*A stripped preproduction vehicle under-slung from a Royal Naval Commando Westland Wessex HU5, at the FVRDE Chertsey in September 1966. (Courtesy REME Museum)*

*The preproduction vehicles were used in airportability trials with various aircraft, here a wooden fuselage mockup is being used to check dimensions. (Courtesy Airborne Forces Museum)*

*Front view of an FFR preproduction vehicle in stripped down form. This clearly shows the four-way tyre mounting strap and the wing light protection plates. Note also the location of the mirrors and the lack of the cut-out in the bonnet for the radio coaxial leads seen on production vehicles. (Courtesy Dunsfold Collection)*

LAND ROVER

*Side view of an FFR preproduction vehicle in stripped down form. Note that the radio table is a standard FFR item, not the production Half-Ton design. Many detail differences to the production vehicles are evident in this photo. (Courtesy Dunsfold Collection)*

*Interior view of an FFR preproduction vehicle. Noteworthy features include the canvas doorcheck straps, the handthrottle design, the twin wiper motors (as on the Rover 8), the lack of flyscreens on the air vents, and the windscreen mounting brackets. (Courtesy Dunsfold Collection)*

LAND
ROVER

*Excellent front study of a preproduction vehicle, this one being an FFR in built up form. Note the way the aerial mounts are fixed. (Courtesy Dunsfold Collection)*

*Not much room inside an Andover. (Courtesy Airborne Forces Museum)*

It was possible, with the reduced width of the new Land Rover, to fit two vehicles abreast inside the Argosy. (Courtesy Airborne Forces Museum)

have lifted that weight anyway! In the end it didn't matter, since Aden, by that time, was being phased out from the British sphere of influence.

The specification also demanded that two vehicles could be placed side by side in the Armstrong Whitworth Argosy aircraft, which had come into service in 1962. It was not possible to fit in two standard Land Rovers. This, therefore, was why the Half-Ton was some 4 inches narrower than the standard Series IIAs of the time. Incidentally, the 109in APGP was not suited for this new specification either, of course, as it was too large and far too heavy.

Right and opposite: The Bristol Britannia, with its side door, was a little more awkward. (Courtesy Airborne Forces Museum)

In 1966, the Armstrong Whitworth Argosy, the Blackburn Beverley, the Bristol Britannia, Shorts' Belfast, the Hawker Siddeley Andover and the Vickers VC10 aircraft made up the transport fleet. Aircraft loading trials were carried out on these aircraft but, by the time the Half-Ton came into service the Beverley had disappeared, and, by early 1969, five squadrons of Lockheed C130 Hercules provided the main tactical airlift capability of the RAF. It was then possible to fit unstripped vehicles into the C130, due to its large size.

The weight specification meant that Land Rover had to lose 450lb (204kg) on the weight of the standard Rover 8 GS, which was its lightest vehicle. It was not really feasible to develop a totally new vehicle, as the initial orders were small. Only 75 were originally intended for the Royal Marines, with small follow-on quantities for the heliportable role. As the engine, transmission and chassis could not be changed greatly, and were proven components, the only really feasible option was to reduce the weight of the body. It also made good logistical

*A well loaded Rover 1 on UN duties emerges from an RAF C130 in Cyprus. (Courtesy Crown Copyright/MoD)*

UNITED NATIONS
LAND ROVER
42 FG 91

LAND ROVER

*VXC 702F. This was the first production vehicle built in 1967. (Courtesy Dunsfold Collection)*

sense to keep as many parts as possible identical to those of the normal Land Rover military fleet.

Land Rover, therefore, came up with the rather ingenious idea of a totally new flat-panelled body, designed to be made with the bare minimum of tooling. This is why it was made from flat and folded panels, and from many small parts spot-welded and riveted together when larger pressings would clearly have been preferable. The only significant press tool was for the bonnet, but even that was made in two pieces to keep the costs down.

The design made it possible to quickly remove the top half of the load bed, the tailgate (which could be split since it consisted of two parts), the doors, the windscreen, and the bumper. Many of these items, along with the spare tyre, would not really be required on the Drop Zone during operations anyway, but could be brought up at

*EXC 890G, seen here at Eastnor Castle in 1969, when almost new, is an early production vehicle which was either chassis number 23600007 or 8. (Courtesy Dunsfold Collection)*

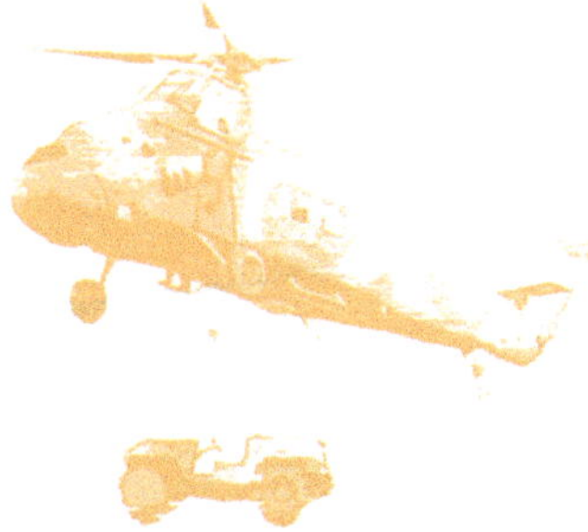

*19 LR 69 is actually a false registration. It is really NXC 25H, a vehicle which was used in a lot of publicity material. (Courtesy Dunsfold Collection)*

ROYAL AIR FORCE
W

***An early Rover 1 is lifted by an RAF Westland Wessex HC2; what it was all about!***
***(Courtesy Dunsfold Collection)***

***Paratroopers with an early Rover 1 in stripped down form.***
***(Courtesy Land Rover***

***Land Rover advert and artist's impression for the Half-Ton, November 1967. (Courtesy Dunsfold Collection)***

***Land Rover brochure for the Rover 1. (Courtesy Dunsfold Collection)***

*Below: The most noticeable change on the Rover 1 was the moving of the headlights from the grill to the wings. Here, a LHD Rover 1 GS in Bronze Green takes part in a military driving competition. (Courtesy Imperial War Museum)*

*Land Rover was also to design a much larger vehicle which looked like a larger Lightweight but this had nothing to do with Project Lightweight. It had a 110in wheelbase with a 2995cc 6 cylinder petrol engine. 2 or 3 were built in 1965 and possibly 1966. (Courtesy John Mastrangelo)*

*CXC 212G, the first production RHD vehicle, was retained by Rover for trials. Seen here in 1990, it is now in the USA. (Author's collection)*

*MXC 682H stripped down and with a unitary radio station fitted, the design of which did not change throughout production of both Rover 1 and Series 3. (Courtesy Dunsfold Collection)*

*The Royal Marines received large numbers of early Rover 1s and, with the second order being for 1000 vehicles, many of these, too, went to the Royal Marines. (Courtesy Royal Marines Museum)*

7
33 FG 97

*An early LHD Rover 1 GS, from the first LHD contract. (Courtesy Imperial War Museum)*

*After the Royal Marines got their vehicles, other units started to get the new Rover 1s. Here, a LHD vehicle of the British Army of the Rhine is seen with Soviet observers in the foreground. (Courtesy Imperial War Museum)*

***This early Rover 1, which was converted to a hardtop, is in NATO Green over-painted in disruptive pattern black. Note that the wheel rims still appear to be in Bronze Green. (Courtesy Ken Porter)***

***A brand new Rover 1, after being flown into Northern Ireland in 1972 by the Lockheed C130 Hercules in the background, shares the apron with a Rover 11. Both vehicles are FFR, LHD, and Bronze Green. (Courtesy Imperial War Museum)***

203
XV203
50 FK 57

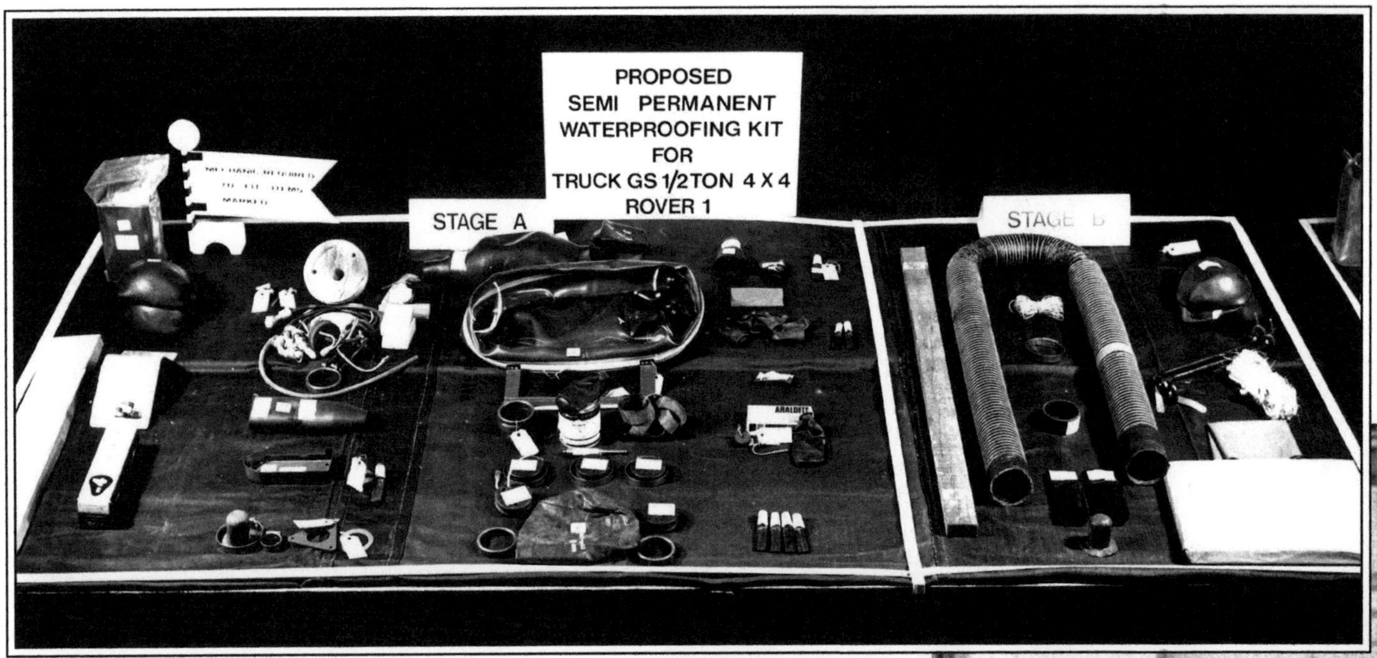


***Waterproofing kit for the Rover 1 GS. (Courtesy REME Museum)***

a later date as a separate load (or so it was argued). A new lighter and narrower bumper was also designed, and the wings were reduced to little more than glorified mudguards. This also had the effect of reducing the outside width to 60in (152.4cm) as opposed to 64in (162.5cm) on the Rover 8 and 10. It was also necessary to make a completely new and narrower bulkhead, with a removable top section, to provide additional clearance inside aircraft. This also saved weight, of course. The axles were fitted with different halfshafts, driving members and end caps, to keep flush with the overall width, while the wheel track remained the same at 511/2in. This was eventually to become the Half-Ton that would be one of the most successful military Land Rovers ever, seeing service from early 1969 to the turn of the century.

## 'Project Truck General Service Lightweight'

**The specifications:**

Lightweight version of short wheelbase Land Rover.

The vehicle had to meet the following requirements:

1) Overall width: 60in maximum.
2) Unladen weight: 2500lb (1135kg) for 12 volt Cargo. 3100lb (1406kg) for 24 volt FFR.
3) Range: 300 miles (482km).
4) Towing: 10cwt trailer (508kg).
5) Lifting points to be provided.
6) Payload: 1000lb (including driver).

Mike Broadhead was the Project Engineer who did the early development work (Norman Busby was his assistant). However, when actual production started, Bob Seager became Project Engineer. The first prototype was built in 1965, and trials began at the FVRDE that same year.

To give an idea of the pains taken to lose weight on pre-production vehicles, the front vent flyscreens were left off some vehicles, as were the rear load area protection strips! Webbing straps with an over centre catch were used to restrain the spare wheel (instead of the normal large metal bracket). 6.00 x 16 tyres were even fitted to the prototype to save weight, along with normal commercial well-base wheel rims instead of the

***Exhibition of the waterproofing kit for the Rover 1 GS. Note the line on the windscreen showing the fording depth of 5 feet. (Courtesy REME Museum)***

*Waterproofed stripped down vehicles drive ashore, without getting wet! (Courtesy Royal Marines Museum)*

standard WD pattern divided wheel rims. Production (and pre-production) vehicles, however, were fitted with 6.50 x 16 tyres. It's not known how many prototypes were actually made, but one carried the military registration 20 BT 90.

On the pre-production FFR vehicles, a standard FFR radio table was fitted (the Half-Ton demountable one was yet to be designed). The oil cooler was omitted on the original specification GS vehicles, but when production began this decision was overturned, and an oil cooler was fitted.

The pre-production vehicles were built on the Rover 8 chassis and were used in many airportability trials, in stripped and unstripped configurations and in various aircraft, to test their suitability in the role.

The Half-Ton in pre-production form made its first official appearance in October 1966, with a completely stripped GS (with 8.20 x 15 sand tyres) and an unstripped FFR being displayed at the FVRDE exhibition at Chertsey. At this time it was still classed as a 1/4 Ton, but, when the production vehicles were built, they were classed as 1/2 Ton.

**Pre-production Vehicles (Rover Mk 1, 1/4 Ton 4x4).**

Contract WV5101 July 1966
Registration numbers:
00 SP 13 became 21 BT 92 then 60 EP 78
00 SP 14 became 21 BT 84 then 60 EP 79
00 SP 15 became 21 BT 85
00 SP 16 became 60 EP 81 then 21 BT 93
00 SP 17 became 21 BT 94
00 SP 18 became 21 BT 95 then 60 EP 80
Most were RHD. For more details see Appendix 1.

In some of the accompanying photos, it is evident that the loss of all of 4in in the overall width makes all the difference in getting two vehicles side by side in an aircraft. The Army Air Transport and Development Centre (AATDC), based at Old Sarum in Wiltshire, initially carried out trials on the new vehicle. In January 1968, however, air trials became the responsibility of JATE (Joint Air Trials Establishment) at Brize Norton.

The first display to the general public was at the Commercial Motor Show at Earls Court in September 1968. Land Rover's accompanying press release stated that: "The Army has already placed orders for the new vehicle, and it is expected that it will gradually succeed the normal 88in Land Rover, which is the standard light 4x4 in its load class, in all British Forces. Several overseas armies have also shown keen interest in the new model. The Lightweight Land Rover can be dropped by parachute from an aircraft and a special air-dropping platform has been developed for the purpose. When the vehicle reaches the ground it can be immediately driven away."

Possible uses, which the Land Rover press release saw for the Lightweight, included: "as a personnel or cargo carrier or in numerous other roles including mobile radio station, recovery vehicle, emergency two-stretcher carrier, mobile workshop and reconnaissance and fire service vehicle."

The pre-production vehicles were classed as 'Truck General Service Lightweight' (also FFR) (Rover Mk 1, 1/4 Ton 4x4).

Land Rover was also to design a much larger vehicle, which looked like a larger Lightweight, but this had nothing to do with Project Lightweight. It had a 110in wheelbase with a 2995cc 6-cylinder petrol engine, and quantity production did not occur, with only 2 or 3 being built in 1965 and possibly 1966. The first one, VXC 100F, survives in the Dunsfold Land Rover Collection.

**Test and Demonstrator Vehicles**

The first prototype was built in 1965, when trials began at the FVRDE.
VXC 702F (the first production LHD vehicle), together with another LHD unregistered vehicle, were built in December 1967.
CXC 212G, which also carried the military registration 20 BT 91, was an FFR, and the first RHD production vehicle built in 1968.
EXC 809G was registered in March 1969.
NXC 25H, an FFR, was displayed in 1970 at the FVRDE exhibition.
MXC 682H was an FFR.
For more details see Appendix 1.

**Production vehicles**

After the completion of the FVRDE trials, which turned out to be successful for Land Rover, the first orders were placed by the MoD in August 1967. These were for 92 vehicles for the Royal Navy (Royal Marines) under contract WV7477, and 1000 vehicles for the Army under contract WV7478, all

T 4
59FG61

61 FK 11

***61 FK 11 stripped down. The wooden strip on the grill is to protect the bonnet from being damaged by the lifting chains. (Courtesy Royal Marines Museum)***

***A well-loaded Rover 1 GS splashes ashore from a landing craft. (Courtesy Royal Marines Museum)***

***As well as the emergency ambulance, standard GS and FFR vehicles were used by medical units. Here, a Rover 1 leads a Humber Pig ambulance out of a base in Ulster in 1975. (Courtesy Royal Marines Museum)***

were GS vehicles. Production started in December 1967, although only two LHD vehicles were completed that year. By 1968, at least 500 had been built (of which only 5 were LHD). The evidence on when the first vehicles actually went into service is somewhat contradictory. The very first vehicles may have entered service in December 1968, but it is clear that in January

*A Rover 1 training vehicle, rigged for deep wading, with the Royal Marines in Poole, Dorset, 1987. (Courtesy REME Museum)*

*Excellent study of a Rover 1 Linelayer showing the equipment in place. (Courtesy REME Museum)*

1969 at least 760 vehicles had been delivered to the MoD, many of these being assigned to the Royal Marines. The first LHD production vehicles were delivered to the MoD in April 1969.

The only real change during production involved moving the headlights from the grill panel to the wings. This seems to have occurred late in 1970, and was due to lighting regulations in those countries in which vehicles could well be used by the British armed forces. This meant that about 1500 models had this arrangement. Only another 1489 would be built before production would switch to the Series 3.

The payload had been increased to a $^{1}/_{2}$ Ton, compared to a $^{1}/_{4}$ Ton for other Land Rover 88in wheelbase 4x4s in service. This, however, did not mean that the new vehicle could carry more, it was just that the Army changed the nomenclature to include the overall payload, and not just the weight it could carry in the load bed. The first User Hand Book (AC 22178) was issued in August 1968.

The second RHD production vehicle was delivered under contract WV7477 to the Royal Marines, with the military registration number 71 FG 97. This vehicle, chassis number 23600002, was built on 20 November 1968 and struck off census in June 1977. It still survives and is undergoing restoration in Edinburgh.

The last (numerically) was 01 FL 14, chassis number 23601881. It was struck off census in November 1979, and was among the last vehicles built in March 1972. (See Appendix 1 for fuller details of contracts). The last 10 RHD vehicles were delivered in April 1972 to 'Crown Agents Jamaica'. The very last RHD production vehicle had chassis number 23601893.

The term 'General Service' in the description of the Rover 1 was dropped in favour of 'Utility' (in March 1972). The latter should not be confused with the 'Truck Utility $^{1}/_{4}$ Ton 4x4 GS Rover Mk 1' (the Series 1 80in wheelbase of 1948-51).

The RAF and RN ordered small quantities of Rover 1 Half-Tons, with the RAF taking 132 between April and June 1969. Royal Navy or Royal Marines vehicles displayed 'RN' registration plates, while RAF vehicles were on 'AA' plates. No foreign forces purchased the Rover 1 Half-Ton from new, but a small number of ex British Army Rover 1 vehicles (believed to be 8) were used by the Cypriot National Guard (EØvikñ Φpoupá). These were fitted with the American M40 106mm recoilless rifle. It is not known if this conversion was carried out when in British service or (more probably) by the Cypriot National Guard.

Around 3000 Series IIA Half-Tons were built, including pre-production and trials vehicles. Many were withdrawn from service in the mid to late 1970s, although others survived until the 1980s and a few lingered on into the 1990s. The last known to be struck off census was in March 1998, despite the fact that the Rover 1 was declared obsolete in April 1987!

The Rover 1 contracts are listed at Appendix 1.

## Half-Ton FFR and GS Production Vehicles - Basic Description

**Identification of Rover 1 GS and FFR.**

Rover 1 GS: Three front seats fitted. Rear bench seats fitted. Rover 1 FFR: Two front seats, centre seat position taken up by battery box cover. Unitary radio kit in rear load bed.

Based on the Rover 10, which it replaced in GS and FFR form, the main difference was the body. The Rover 1 fulfilled the same role as the Rover 8 and 10, but could be reduced in weight and bulk quickly, resulting in a plain but useful vehicle for air transportation.

The following would be removed from the basic vehicle for helicopter air lifting: doors, tailgate, upper body panels, hood and sticks, rear seats, spare wheel and windscreen. The front bumper (No. 1 crossmember) could also be removed. The chassis, which had an overall width of 60in, was modified by the addition of an angled strip of metal welded across the front chassis legs. The purpose of this was to strengthen the front of the chassis when the bumper was removed, otherwise the chassis flexed too much. Incidentally, vehicle registration numbers were often stencilled onto the No. 1 crossmember.

The standard springs on the Rover 8 and 10 were replaced by lighter road springs, with only 7 leaves on both the front and rear axles. The Half-Ton GS, however, had only 5 leaves on the front.

Vehicles were delivered with a special grab rail for the rear, which fitted into place in a bracket on the rear bulkhead and into a round hole in the lower tailgate. This was for troops to hang onto once the body was stripped down (otherwise there was nothing). This rail clipped onto the rear bulkhead for stowage when not in use.

A NATO rotating/lockable tow hook (FV332151) was fitted to the rear crossmember, with provision for one to be fitted onto the front bumper. Bumperettes were fitted front and rear so that the vehicle could push start another of the same type in all combinations of loading conditions. Lifting rings were also provided.

The gearbox crossmember (No. 4) was detachable, to enable easier replacement of the gearbox, and the gearbox oil filler was at the top. The axles had shorter halfshafts and drive flanges (than the 8 and 10) which reduced the outside width to 60in (152.4cm) as opposed to 64in (162.5cm).

The electrical system had to be to the approved FVRDE standards, except for the numberplate light. This meant that all wiring was to strict specifications; for example, tropicalised harness and fittings, with waterproofed lamps. This meant that all Rover 1s had the same military pattern lights as were fitted to most Service vehicles at the time, not commercial pattern lights. A 6-way light switch was fitted, along with a rear convoy light for tactical night driving.

FFR 24 volt vehicles had a screened distributor, sparking plugs and ignition coil, along with screened and armoured cables for the charging circuit. The

***Rear view of a Rover 1 Linelayer. (Courtesy REME Museum)***

20
41FG96

***41 FG 96 newly fitted with an unpainted Northern Ireland Vehicle Protection Kit. (Courtesy REME Museum)***

*Wombat, front view, in 1969.*
*(Courtesy Royal Marines Museum)*

9
ATKG
72 FG 56
2

LAND ROVER
72 FG 02
9
ATK3

*Wombat, rear view. (Courtesy Royal Marines Museum)*

| | Rover 1 GS | Rover 1 FFR | Rover 8 GS | Rover 8 FFR |
|---|---|---|---|---|
| ***With 20 gallons of fuel and coolant*** | | | | |
| Unladen | 3210lb (1456kg) | 3514lb (1593kg) | 3220lb (1461kg) | 3690lb (1674kg) |
| Laden (max) | 4453lb (2020kg) | 4453lb (2020kg) | 4453lb 2020kg | 4453lb (2020kg) |
| ***With 5 gallons of fuel and no spare wheel*** | | | | |
| Stripped Unladen | 2660lb (1206kg) | 2810lb (1274kg) | | |
| Stripped Laden | 3596lb (1631kg) | 3596lb (1631kg) | | |

***Official weights.***

latter consisted of a generator (No. 10 Mk 2), generator panel (No. 9 Mk 3), and a shunt box for the ammeter.

Suppression of radio interference was to FVRDE Specification 2051, i.e. fully suppressed, bonded and screened. Rover 1 FFRs were ready to accept the Larkspur radio system.

Dunlop Trakgrip 6.50 x 16 tyres were fitted as standard. No heater was fitted on the production line to earlier vehicles, but some vehicles were later modified by the Services to include heaters, and very late vehicles had them factory fitted.

All vehicles were undersealed from new to FVRDE standards. All had a two-piece tailgate, with stowage provision for a pick and shovel. Other stowage provided included the spare wheel carrier on the bonnet, and rifle clips on the bulkhead. The starting and jack handles were fitted under the bonnet, and the jack was accommodated in the rear tool locker on the left-hand side.

The rear numberplate was fixed on a hinged assembly on the lower part of the tailgate. This was so that it would still be visible when the tailgate was down. A commercial light was fitted, since the standard military numberplate light was too deep for the hinged numberplate support. Later, when the MoD did a huge study on cost reductions on their other Land Rover models, the only recommendation to be carried out was a change to a commercial numberplate light.

A second reason for fitting the rear numberplate on the lower part of the tailgate was so that the upper half could be removed for airportability.

Two 10-gallon fuel tanks were fitted, with under-seat filling.

**Official Titles and Asset Vehicle Codes of the Series IIA Half-Ton.**

FVRDE classification was FV18101 (GS), FV18102 (FFR).

Truck, General Service, 1/2 Ton, 4x4, Rover 1. Codes were 1620-0772 (RHD) and 1620-5772 (LHD).

Truck, General Service, FFR, 1/2 Ton 4x4, Rover 1. Codes were 1625-0772 (RHD) and 1625-5772 (LHD).

See also Appendix 1.

**Official Weights**

The FFR was fitted with a quickly demountable modular radio kit (see under "FFR fittings" below). The Rover 1 was rated to carry 896lb (406kg), plus driver and passenger, off road. Towing capacity was rated at 2462lb (1117kg).

If one studies the weights in the accompanying table, it can be seen how useful the vehicle was in the late 1960s, even if the actual weight loss (compared to the Rover 8 and 10 models) was quite small. Later, larger and more capable helicopters and aircraft would make the Half-Ton obsolete in its original design form.

## Generating System and Ignition - FFR vehicles

**Description of Ignition System**

As most military radio equipment required a negative earth 24 volt supply, this was provided on the FFR version, and incorporated a screened and waterproofed ignition system. The Lucas coil was, in fact, a 10 volt oil-filled unit, the voltage being

***Wombat in action. (Courtesy Royal Marines Museum)***

Wombat, view from above.
(Courtesy Royal Marines Museum)

***A Rover 1 gets recovered. (Courtesy REME Museum)***

***The last Rover 1s were built in early 1972 when the Series 3 was introduced. Here, a Rover 1 leads an early Series 3 off a landing craft. (Courtesy Royal Marines Museum)***

dropped down from 24 volts via the filter unit which was used to suppress interference to radio equipment. This filter consisted of a choke, connected in series with two resistors to the coil, and two capacitors connected one across each end of the choke to earth.

The Lucas DZS 4A distributor was a screened unit mounted on an extension of the fuel pump drive shaft. It had an automatic centrifugal advance mechanism, with an operating range of 0 to 22 degrees over a distributor speed range of 750 to 2400rpm (engine speed of 1500 to 4800rpm). Spark plugs were 14mm (3/4in) reach, with a built-in 1000-3000 ohm resistor which suppressed radio interference and reduced the burning rate of the central electrode.

**Description of Generating System**

To meet the heavy demands of 24 volt equipment, FFR vehicles had a 24 volt 90 amp generator, together with a rectifier system and generator panel. The whole vehicle system, including lighting, was therefore 24 volts. The system allowed for a high generator output to be obtained even at low engine revolutions. Provision was made to charge the batteries when the vehicle was stationary, by the use of a hand throttle control. The hand throttle could be used to increase engine speed to give an ideal charging rate.

Running the generator with the batteries disconnected resulted in the generation of a very high voltage and, if this occurred, the rectifier units would be destroyed. Likewise, faulty connections within the charging circuit would cause voltage surges, with the same effect. A warning plate was fixed to the driver's side seat box stating that the engine must never be run with the vehicle batteries disconnected or with faulty connections in the charging circuit.

**Generator No. 10 Mk 2 90 amp (FV546125)**

The 24 volt negative earth electrical system fitted on FFR vehicles comprised an alternating current 90 amp generator (fully suppressed, partially waterproofed, and ventilated by a 7 inch fan). It was a self-excited 3-phase alternator with a built-in rectifier system. Generating 24 volts at a cutting-in speed of 950rpm it attained its maximum output of 27.5 volts at 90 amperes at 1900rpm (1070rpm engine speed).

**Generator panel No. 9 Mk 3 (FV546131)**

The No. 9 Mk 3 generator panel was used in combination with the above generator. It was a cast aluminium box, with a cover, bolted to a bracket behind the rear right-hand bulkhead, and it housed the control units for the generator. The box had two compartments, the partition between them acted, along with suppressing capacitors, as a radio interference screen. One compartment housed a heavy-duty relay and the other had a vibrating contact regulator, along with its associated resistors (which were used to control the voltage of the generator). It also housed a high/low voltage setting link (low setting used in tropical climates) and radio suppression filters.

The relay in the first compartment connected the radio batteries in parallel with the vehicle batteries so they would be charged when the generator had obtained the required output. The operating coil of the relay was connected to the auxiliary rectified output terminal of the generator. Two pairs of contacts were fitted to the relay, and were used to connect the positive line of the generator to the vehicle battery positive connection and to the radio battery positive connection, respectively, when the relay closed.

**Shunt Box**

A shunt box was fitted on the rear left-hand side of the seat bulkhead. As well as accommodating the shunts, this provided terminals to allow connection to the vehicle and radio batteries. A shunt is a precision resistor used in conjunction with an ammeter. It allows most of the current to be drawn through the shunt whilst at the same time allowing the associated ammeter to indicate current flow. This means that the ammeter wiring carried a low current and, therefore, could be fairly compact. Without shunts, the high currents encountered would dictate much thicker wiring to carry the required current.

Two ammeters were provided on the dashboard to monitor the current being drawn (or supplied) for both the radio and vehicle batteries.

**Operation of the 90 amp Generating System**

Starting the vehicle by the key completed the field circuit through the closed contacts of the relay and of the regulator, within the generator panel. As the engine was started and engine speed increased, the generated voltage rose and, when it reached 18 to 20 volts, the relay closed and the generator positive line was connected to the vehicle and radio batteries. The rate of charge of both sets of batteries was shown by the two ammeters in the instrument panel.

When the generated voltage reached 28.5 to 29 volts, the regulator contacts opened to insert a resistance in the field circuit, the voltage fell and the regulator contacts closed again. This cycle repeated itself rapidly and continuously until the speed of the generator was reduced and the voltage was below the regulator operating voltage.

This system was used on the previous Rover 8 FFR (late vehicles), which the Rover 1 replaced, and was used with minor modifications up until the last Series 3 FFR vehicles were built.

**FFR Fittings**

All FFR vehicles were fitted with a unitary radio kit, featuring a radio table which also housed the batteries. There was provision for four 90 amp/hour UK/6/TN batteries, although

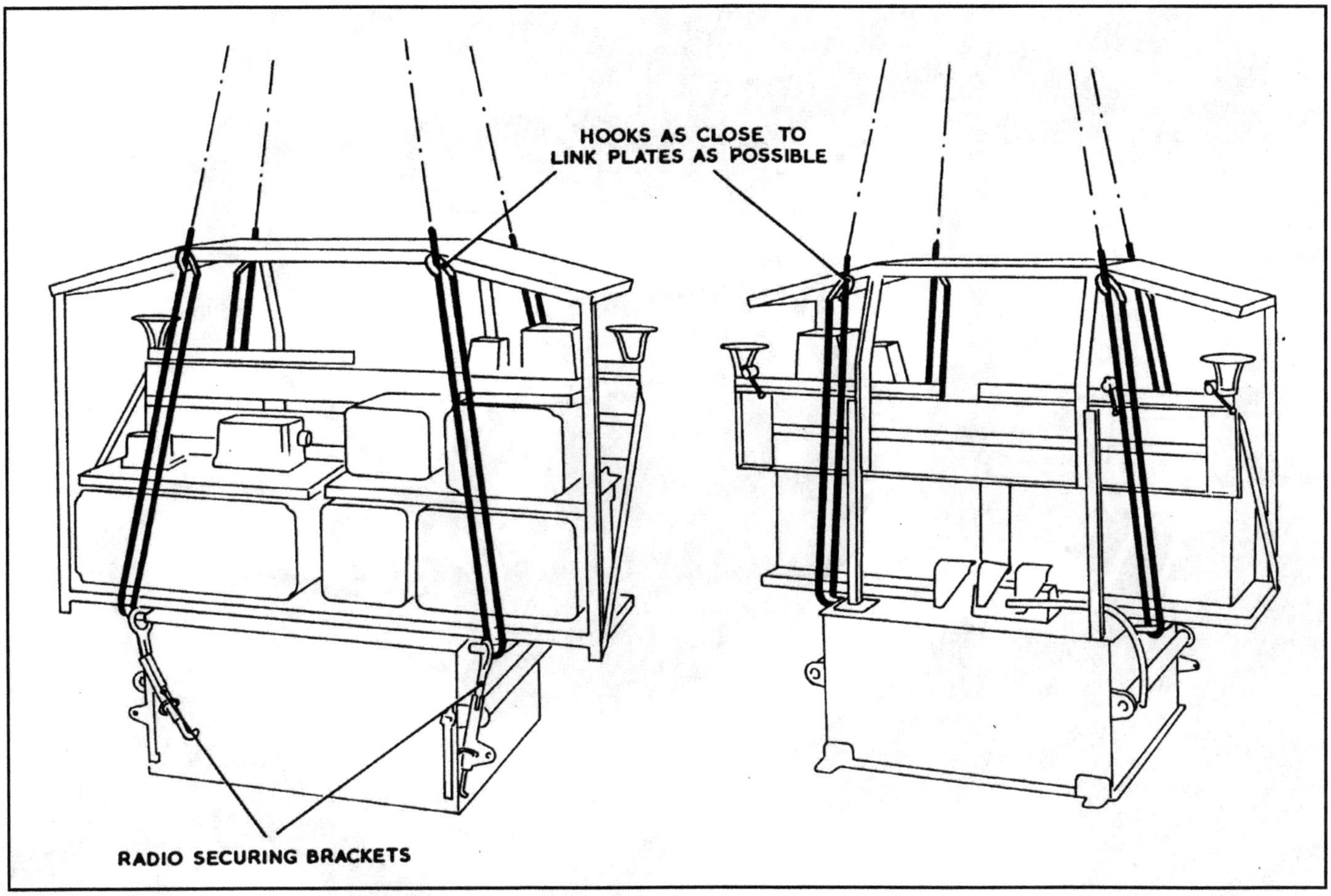


***Unitary Radio Station showing rigging for helicopter lifting.***

normally only two were fitted. There were two fibreglass battery boxes clamped to trays which could be slid out for maintenance. Each box held a pair of batteries. The boxes were not necessary for the installation, but were intended to catch any acid spillage during airporting. The kit had to totally replicate the fixed installations on all other FFR Land Rovers, with the relationship between the table and the racking being the same. This meant that radio installations were identical across the fleet.

A Dexion framework, to which radios, junction boxes and other radio paraphernalia were bolted, was part of the installation. This frame also had two sliding aerial brackets attached on the top section, with four special quick-release clamps. These brackets could be protruded through the canvas sides, via special flaps. A metal mesh canopy was provided to protect the radio installation from possible damage caused by the slings being released during helicopter operations. A set of holes was provided in the centre of the metal canopy to mount an aerial base, if required, though this was rarely used.

As the unit was self contained, being charged via the vehicle's electrical system, it was possible to quickly release it from its mounting and install it into another vehicle (if the original carrying vehicle was disabled, for example, or if it was necessary to convert the vehicle into a cargo vehicle).

Alternatively, the radio modular unit was demountable and airportable, with the mesh cage protecting the installation when lifting by helicopter. It could also be used as a ground station, relying on the batteries within the set. The two radio operators' seats had fold down legs for use when outside the vehicle. The Royal Marines, for instance, transferred the set into modified 3/4 ton trailers, to give greater tactical flexibility (the trailer installation carried its own generator for battery charging). The FFR vehicles fitted with this unit were certainly not light, as the unitary kit weighed in at 184lb (83kg) plus the weight of the actual radio kit!

Bob Seager recalls, "The design and development of the unitary radio kit was a surprisingly complicated business. One problem was securing it to the vehicle. We bought some rather expensive catches, which were ideal but, unfortunately, chrome plated. We sent them to our lab to be stripped, but someone forgot them, and by next morning they had dissolved! After that

***Opposite: The rear of a Rover 1 FFR. A Royal Marine entertains a little girl with the radio. (Courtesy Royal Marines Museum)***

we made a turnbuckle device, but found that, when we tightened them, the body sides pulled in to meet the kit. Eventually, a brainstorming session (that's a chat down the pub) produced a design that would secure the kit but could not be over tightened.

"Wiring was a major project. To make it readily demountable, quick release connectors had to be used, and loose leads were unacceptable, since, with live batteries in the kit and a live charging circuit, the scope for major short circuits was obvious. Proprietary plugs and sockets were either to aircraft standard and ferociously expensive, or commercial standard and not robust, and a special design was eventually produced for us.

"The kit incorporated quite a lot of ingenious design features, mainly to the credit of Graham Fazackerly, one of my technical assistants. It was manufactured by DCM Products Ltd. at Coventry."

## Rover 1 Variants

All vehicles were built as soft tops, with both left and right-hand drive versions, though a small number were subsequently converted to hard tops. As we have seen, there were two basic versions: the 12 volt, General Service (GS) used as a personnel carrier and general cargo transport vehicle, and the 24 volt, Fitted For Radio (FFR). The latter had provision for charging additional batteries from the vehicle

***Close-up of the Dexion framework with a bracket for the aerial mount. (Author's collection)***

72 FG 59

***Rover 1 GS, RAF Mountain Rescue. The bonnet is yellow in common with other RAF Mountain Rescue vehicles. The RAF ordered small quantities of Rover 1 Half-Tons, taking 132 between April and June 1969. (Courtesy Ken Porter)***

***This vehicle was one of the 92 built in the first contract. The view clearly shows that the top half of the tailgate is removable. This photograph was taken in Northern Ireland in 1969. (Courtesy Royal Marines Museum)***

system, which could then be used to power radio stations, for example, or other applications needing a 24 volt independent power supply.

**Amphibious Half-Ton**

An interesting application of the Rover 1 Half-Ton was that used by the Royal Marines and other units which developed a way of driving ashore from landing craft in depths up to 5 feet (1.524 metres). This was done by using special water-proofing conversion kits comprising elastic waterproof covers, PVC bags, rubber bungs, battery vent covers, rubber non-return valves, etc. Various types of sealant and other materials were also used, such as Scotch tape No. 33 (for sealing PVC bags), Bostik 1261 or 1262, Prestikon (plastic sealing compound), Wading fabric No. 2, sisal rope, and baling twine.

To enable a vehicle to be used either as a normal road vehicle, or in the wading role, the kit was applied in three stages. Land Rovers were fitted with most of the kit at Stage 1, and this imposed no limitations on vehicle use. This would take at least 14 hours to do. Stage 2, which took an hour, involved checking all previous work carried out, making sure the fuel tanks were full, minor greasing of components, fitting a towrope, and ensuring all kit was packed in PVC bags and stowed away. This would take place just before embarkation. Stage 3 involved rechecking the above, fitting tailboard stays to ensure quick flooding of the vehicle, and final finishing of sealing and greasing of some minor items.

The stages of waterproofing would be indicated with three 3in x 1in oblong colour codes on the front off-side wing (blue, yellow and red). A blue oblong, for example, denoted that stage 1 was completed. The oblong codes not in use were covered with masking tape.

Once the Land Rover left the landing craft, it was driven without changing gear and at a high engine speed to prevent stalling in low gear and four wheel drive.

Today, the Royal Marines have a facility in Devon called the Amphibious Trials and Training Unit Royal Marines (ATTURM), which is used to train personnel in this role. The unit was formed in June 1979 from the Amphibious Experimental Establishment (AXE) and the Fording Trials Branch (FTB) REME.

A way of telling if this modification has been done is to look for a large plugged hole (about 25/8in diameter) on the left-hand side of the bulkhead, below the heater motor. This was where the carburettor breather pipe (Q-hose) ran up to the windscreen. Vehicles often had a front bumper-mounted NATO tow hook for self-recovery.

**Emergency Ambulance**

The Half-Ton could be converted for use as a forward emergency ambulance by fitting an extra canvas tilt and racking for two stretchers. The ride, however, must have been a little rough and uncomfortable.

**Line Layer**

For the communications role, Rover 1 Land Rovers were modified to dispense D10 twisted cable (landline) over long distances. These were for use with field telephones, for example, linking unit sections to a command post or section commander.

The installation kit fitted to the Half-Ton was a similar version to that designed and fitted to the Rover 8.

The vehicle could carry eleven miles of D10 cable, four miles of which was carried in the dispenser racks located in the rear of the vehicle, one on each side. By pre-jointing each 1/2 mile pack in the racks, it was possible to lay a two mile route. Cable could also be dispensed from an 'Apparatus Cable Laying' (basically a large cable drum), mounted in the rear load bed, but at a much slower speed than from the dispenser racks. There was, however, some variety in the equipment fitted; for instance some had two cable dispensers in the rear, whilst some had one outside the vehicle. A special shortened canvas tilt was fitted to give some protection to the driver, even though many vehicles had their doors removed. A rack was fitted between the middle seats for the crew's 9mm sub-machine guns.

The superstructure was designed to accommodate a ladder, telegraph poles and crooksticks (similar to shepherds' crooksticks, but for retrieving the wire). Two tool bins were located in the rear of the vehicle for stowage of loose tools, such as shovels and hammers. Later Series 3 vehicles were also used in this role.

**81mm Mortar**

A small number of Rover 1s were converted to carry the 81mm mortar

and were used by the Parachute Regiment. The 81mm L16 mortar had a crew of three, a range of 5600 metres, and could fire HE, smoke and practice rounds. The weight of the mortar in the firing position was 36.6kg.

**Vehicle Protection Kit**

In Northern Ireland from 1971, Land Rovers, including Rover 1s, were fitted with the Northern Ireland Vehicle Protection Kit (VPK) made from Glass Reinforced Plastic (GRP) panels to protect vehicles and their occupants. For a comprehensive description of the VPKs see Chapter 3.

**Wombat**

Some Rover 1 Half-Tons were modified in 1969 by fitting the lightweight anti-tank Wombat, BAT, L6, 120mm recoilless rifle. This fired a High Explosive Squash Head (HESH) projectile, with a tactical range of 25 to 1000 metres. An M8C .50in spotting rifle, which had similar trajectories, using M48 tracer rounds (20 rounds/magazine) was fitted, to show when the main weapon was on target. This was ascertained by the presence of a small burst of smoke on the target when hit. This was important, as a very conspicuous back blast could well be visible, giving the Land Rover's position away to the intended target! The danger area behind the recoilless rifle comprised a 30-degree cone from the breech. Anyone within 14 metres needed to be under cover. It was recommended personnel should stay at least 91 metres from the danger area.

The main weapon, with a projectile weight of 27.3kg (60lb), was fired electrically. It was permitted in a wartime scenario to fire the weapon from the vehicle in an arc of 75 degrees. In the user handbook, however, it was stressed that in peace time the gun's main armament should not be fired, as continuous firing would cause damage to the carrying vehicle. Instead, the weapon would be demounted for live firing. For training purposes, the spotting rifle should be used instead.

Wombat weighed 294kg (650lb), and the Royal Marines were among the users of this equipment.

The principle behind the modern recoilless rifle is that the propellant charge is much larger (about 80% larger) than is required to project the shell, the surplus propellant gases being vented to the rear thus cancelling out the rearwards momentum of the fired projectile. The advantages are that the weapon can be relatively light and there is no need for a heavy recoil system or substantial carriage mounting. The drawbacks, however, are that muzzle velocity cannot be high, and the weapon will have a prominent 'firing signature'. The adaptation, however, did offer a very effective mobile light anti-tank capability. The Wombat could, of course, be towed behind a vehicle.

For air transporting Wombat-equipped Half-Tons in the Armstrong Whitworth Argosy aircraft, it was normal to remove the Wombat's venturi.

British BAT weapons were declared obsolete in 1984.

# 2 SERIES 3

The 'Series 3 Truck Half-Ton FFR and GS' was to prove to be a very successful vehicle, in that no standard Series 3 88in wheelbase commercial bodied vehicles were produced (at least for British forces) as FFR or GS vehicles. However, several hundred were procured as basic specification commercial models called Half-Ton CL (Commercial Logistic). These had the minimum modifications for military use which consisted of the addition of a NATO towing hook and associated wiring for a NATO trailer socket. Very large numbers of FFR and GS Half-Tons, however, were ordered by the Army to replace earlier Land Rovers, such as the Rover 8 and 10 1/4 Ton vehicles.

The Royal Navy and Royal Air Force also took orders for reasonable numbers of the CL model, but most vehicles in the half-ton class would be the GS and FFR variants.

The Land Rover Series 3 was introduced in October 1971. However, the Half-Ton Series 3 was not to be introduced into military service until May 1972, when the second production RHD vehicle was delivered to the Central Vehicle Depot at Hilton. This was because Land Rover was still building Rover 1 vehicles in March 1972. The first RHD Series 3, chassis number 95100001A, had been built in early April 1972, and went to Land Rover's Engineering Department. The first LHD Series 3 (chassis 95400001A) was built on 9 May 1972.

The Series 3 was mechanically similar to the Series IIA. Innovations included a new all synchromesh gearbox (with changed ratios), a change to the larger 91/2in clutch plate, and from a dynamo to an alternator on 12 volt vehicles. The Series 3 also had servo assisted brakes (not on early CL models), full width fascia styling (i.e. a dashboard in front of the driver), and many more plastic components. The Series 3 Half-Ton, however, kept the old style dashboard.

Later Rover 1s, of course, had the headlights moved to the wings. This made it hard to tell late IIA vehicles from early Series 3 vehicles, at least from the outside.

By the time the Series 3 was taken into service, though, the design was almost redundant for its original role of a helicopter airportable lightweight vehicle, because more capable aircraft had come into service. It became unusual, therefore, to see vehicles stripped down to the bare minimum.

The Series 3 Half-Ton was produced in much larger numbers than the Rover 1 Half-Ton, and was to see service with many other countries apart from the UK. In the British Armed Forces, from its introduction into service, it was utilised in many different roles and rapidly became the standard vehicle in the Half-Ton class.

From the late 1980s onwards, the Land Rover 90 was to gradually replace it, but it was only effectively replaced at the end of 1997, when the decision to replace all the Series 3 vehicles was taken. Some, however, actually survived in use until the early half of 1999. The last Solihull vehicles were made in late 1984, and went into service in early 1985.

***Lightweights were often used to teach service personnel to drive. (Courtesy Crown Copyright/MoD)***

***Half-Tons were very popular vehicles for use in Army rallying and trials. From a military viewpoint, this was good team training since map reading on the move, often at night, and the ability to drive safely and confidently was an asset to any unit. This shows a trial in 1975. (Courtesy REME Museum)***

58 FL 35

***1972 Series 3 Station Wagon on the Commercial Logistic (CL) chassis. This was basically a civilian model with minimum modifications for military use. Fairly large numbers of CL vehicles were purchased by the MoD, most being soft tops. Some were diesel anti-spark vehicles. (Courtesy Ken Porter)***

## Half-Ton FFR and GS Production Vehicles - Basic Description

### Identification of Series 3 GS and FFR

Series 3 FFR: Two front seats, centre seat position taken up by battery box cover. Unitary radio kit in rear load bed. Series 3 GS: Three front seats fitted. Rear bench seats fitted.

Being based on the Rover 1, it's no surprise that the Series 3 shared many features with the earlier model. The same structures could be removed for helicopter airlifting, i.e., doors, tailgate, upper body panels, hood and sticks, rear seats, spare wheel and windscreen, if required. As was the case for the Rover 1, the front bumper (No. 1 crossmember) could also be removed, and the chassis was modified in the same way to prevent excessive chassis flexing. The chassis had an overall width of 60in, and the standard springs used on the normal Series 3 CL vehicles were replaced by lighter road springs, having only 7 leaves on both front and rear axles (except for the GS which had 5 leaves on the front).

Vehicles were delivered with the special grab rail, which again fitted into place in a bracket on the rear bulkhead and into a round hole in the lower tailgate. As with the Rover 1, this was so there was something for troops to hold onto when the vehicle was stripped down. When the Series 3 came into service, however, it was rarely stripped down to the point where this item would be needed since more

***00 WA 25 - an early Series 3 FFR trials vehicle at Chertsey. (Courtesy REME Museum)***

S60S

LAND ROVER
00 WA 25

*00 WA 25 - an early Series 3 FFR trials vehicle at Chertsey. (Courtesy REME Museum)*

*Series 3 brochure. (Courtesy Dunsfold Collection)*

ROYAL NAVY
26 RN 74

ARMY FIRE SERVICE
46 FL 29

***Royal Navy Series 3 Half-Ton CL. Some of the Half-Ton CL vehicles were diesels. (Courtesy Ken Porter)***

powerful helicopters and aircraft were then in service. It clipped onto the rear bulkhead for stowage when not in use.

Just as with the Rover 1, the NATO rotating/lockable tow hook was fitted to the rear crossmember, with provision for one to be fitted onto the front bumper too. Bumperettes were fitted front and rear, along with lifting rings.

The gearbox crossmember (No. 4) was again detachable, enabling quick changing of the gearbox, which also had the oil filler at the top. The axles were fitted with the new shorter halfshafts and drive flanges which, as was the case with the Rover 1, had the effect of reducing the outside width to 60in (152.4cm) as opposed to 64in (162.5cm).

The electrical system was to approved Military Vehicles and Engineering Establishment (MVEE) standards, of course, which meant that all wiring, except for the numberplate light, was to strict specifications, i.e. tropicalised harness and fittings, with waterproofed lamps. The Series 3, therefore, had the same military pattern lights as fitted to most Service vehicles at the time. A 6 way light switch was fitted along with a convoy light for tactical night driving.

The FFR 24 volt vehicles had the screened distributor, sparking plugs, and ignition coil, along with screened and armoured cables for the charging circuit, the control panel for the alternator, and a shunt box for the ammeter. Suppression of radio interference was to MVEE standards (Specification 2051), i.e. fully suppressed, bonded and screened. Series 3 FFRs were ready to accept the Larkspur radio system. Dunlop Trakgrip (later Goodyear XtraGrip) 6.50 x 16 tyres were fitted as standard.

All Series 3s were undersealed from new to MVEE standards (Specification 2012). All had a two piece tailgate, with stowage provision for a pick and shovel. Other stowage available included the spare wheel carrier on the bonnet and rifle clips on the bulkhead. The starting and jack handles were stored under the bonnet, whilst the jack was kept in the rear tool locker on the left hand side.

The rear numberplate was fixed on a hinged assembly on the lower part of the tailgate. Two 10-gallon fuel tanks were fitted, with under-seat filling.

**Detail Differences from Rover 1**

The major changes, as I have already mentioned, were mechanical (gearbox, clutch, etc.). However, other detail changes included a new type of front bulkhead top with revised windscreen hinges, a change to electrically operated windscreen washer pump, and the wiper motor cover was now plastic instead of aluminium. The horn and headlight dip were now on the headlamp dip and indicator stalk, as opposed to the wheel horn push and floor headlight dip switch on the Rover 1. Ignition was now key start, rather than the old push button start.

New items (factory fitted) included a Smiths heater, which was fitted on the bulkhead above the gearbox tunnel. New fittings included a Hella hazard warning switch, and a brake system warning light and check button. This checked that the brake system was satisfactory by warning of any lack of vacuum from the brake servo, or a loss of brake fluid from the system.

An infra-red headlight switch was fitted which, when on, cut-out all electric lights, including the brake lights, leaving only the headlamps working. The idea was that special infra red filters were fitted over the headlamps, giving out (to the naked eye at least) invisible light. The driver would then wear special filtered goggles which made the infra-red light visible. This system was also used, by unit modification, on the Rover 1.

Early Series 3 vehicles retained the early style halfshafts, flush to body width (see vehicle description above). This feature was to disappear on very late Series 3 production vehicles because the width of the vehicles was no longer relevant (larger aircraft, such as the Lockheed C130 Hercules, the Boeing Chinook and Westland Sea King helicopters, having replaced those for which the Half-Ton had originally been designed).

The first Army Series 3 vehicle into military service (numerically) seems to have been a right hand drive GS, registration number 45 FL 36 (chassis number 95100003A). It was struck off

***46 FL 29 is from the first Army contract for Series 3 vehicles, and is still in factory specification. It has Winguard mirrors and is in factory finish Bronze Green, with a yellow bridge plate and galvanized bumper. (Courtesy Ken Porter)***

***From 1980 on, minor detail changes included: mirrors moved to doors and rear fog lights fitted. This is a Scots Guards' vehicle photographed in 1991. (Author's collection)***

census in December 1977.

The last into service was a right hand drive, RAF, 24 volt, 90 amp vehicle, which carried the registration number 05 KD 65. This vehicle went into service in January 1985 and served with the Red Arrows until April 1994. The Army and RAF contracts are listed at Appendix 1.

The Royal Navy also ordered Series 3 Half-Tons, but details on RN vehicles are not known. Some Royal Navy or Royal Marines vehicles had 'RN' registration plates.

Early RAF vehicles were on 'AM' and 'AJ' plates normally, but, from early 1982, vehicles came within the new unified registration series starting with 'KA'.

**Official Titles and Asset Vehicle Codes of the Series 3 Half-Ton.**

FVRDE classification was FV18103 (GS), FV18104 (FFR).

1) 'Truck, Utility, General Service, 1/2 Ton, 4X4, Rover Series 3'. Codes were 1620-0778 (RHD) and 1620-5778 (LHD).

2) 'Truck, Utility, FFR (Fitted for Radio) 1/2 Ton, 4X4, Rover Series 3'. Codes were 1625-0778 (RHD) and 1625-5778 (LHD).

Both of these had the 2286cc petrol engine. Incidentally, no British versions ever used the 2286cc diesel engine, though two RHD petrol vehicles were converted by Land Rover to LHD, 12 volt 2286cc diesels (for possible use by the RAF), but were never delivered.

Unlike the previous Series IIA, no standard commercial bodied Series 3 88in wheelbase vehicles were produced as GS or FFR, but basic 12 volt commercial models were obtained in relatively small numbers, and the commonest variant was classed as 'basic vehicle'.

3) 'Truck Utility CL 1/2 Ton, 4x4 w/ trailer attachments Series 3 (p)'. Codes were 1621-0778 (RHD) and 1621-5778 (LHD). This was a commercial vehicle with trailer attachments (NATO hook), and a petrol engine.

There were, of course, other variants and codes, of which quite large numbers were delivered. One such variant, known as an Anti Spark vehicle, had spark arrestors in the

exhaust system. This was designed for use in fuel and ammunition dumps to tow weapons trolleys.

The User Hand Book (AC 22228) was issued in May 1972.

Weights remained the same as for the Rover 1.

## Detail Differences Between Early and Late Series 3

### General Changes

During production of the Series 3, there were only detail changes to the model. In about 1975, the front road springs on GS vehicles were replaced by those used on the FFR vehicles, i.e. 7 leaves on the front instead of 5. Around the same time the small glass light lenses on the side, tail and indicator lights were changed to plastic lenses with a new pattern. These gave much better light output without requiring the actual bulb specification to be changed, and started to appear in about 1975 on new vehicles. They were often fitted retrospectively on older Service vehicles.

From about 1977, bridge plates were no longer fitted, as they were no longer in use. Later, in 1979, the location of the washer bottle and pump was changed from the bulkhead to inside the engine bay (the design was also changed). The washer jet nozzles moved from the bulkhead (where they were next to the wipers), onto the bonnet. The toolbox moved inside the engine bay too, from its position by the LH rear wheelarch, again in about 1979.

1980 saw a number of changes to the Series 3, one of which (in October) was the introduction of rear fog lamps. That year also saw the mirrors changed from being wing mounted to door mounted. Other changes in 1980 included the move to electrical sender units for the oil, water and fuel gauges, as opposed to the capillary type. Anti burst door locks were fitted on later vehicles as an improvement on the slam type, since the early slam types were not lockable. Retrofitting these new locks on earlier vehicles was a common modification. The seat base assemblies were also improved in 1980 by the addition of angle brackets to stop them from sliding around. From about 1981, the rear numberplate was moved from the centre of the tailgate to one side, and the lower tailgate now had plain bottom halves without the numberplate bracket and cable hole. Some very late vehicles did not even have the pioneer tools brackets fitted at all. It should be noted that the numberplates on early vehicles had often been moved to the side of the tailgate. This was done for a number of reasons, such as when tailgates were removed in Northern Ireland, for example, or when the vehicles were converted for Wombat.

Seatbelts were changed from static to inertia in June 1981, and a seat rail mounting was added on top of the seat bulkhead. Very late vehicles had a new plastic Land Rover logo badge, and many did not have front bumperettes or the lifting eyes fitted. From 1995 BCF (Bromochlorodifluoromethane) fire extinguishers were gradually exchanged for a new type, due to the Montreal Protocol banning the use of ozone-depleting chemicals. This meant that a new type of bracket had to be fitted for the new larger extinguisher. However, not all vehicles got the new type extinguisher after this date since the modification was not considered to be urgent.

It should be noted that early vehicles were often updated by fitting later parts, or by exchanging components. Because of this, a vehicle may look newer than it really is.

### FFR Vehicles Detail Differences

From 1978 the generator changed from the No. 10 Mk 2 to the No. 10 Mk 3 (FV760740) and the generator panel from the No. 9 Mk 3 to the No. 9 Mk 4 (FV760735) transistorised. These were not interchangeable between sets. Shunt boxes were moved that year, from the rear of the vehicle bulkhead to the middle seat back, and now had a single ammeter incorporated into the shunt box, rather than the two on the dashboard. Early vehicles may well have been modified with the later type of generator and generator panel. For a description of the FFR generating and ignition system see Chapter 1. The operation was similar to the early system, except that switching to a reduced output was now controlled by a transistor rather than an electromechanical regulator.

The generator charging system leads also changed slightly that year, and the location of the amphenol socket was moved from the rear of the seat bulkhead to the front, next to the relocated shunt box. Some vehicles had the generator panel mounted

*Interior view of a Series 3 in Northern Ireland. This vehicle was an ex-VPK returned to its normal role as an FFR vehicle with a TA Signals unit. It has an early Land Rover 90/110 style doortop and late pattern fire extinguisher. (Courtesy Tom Finlay)*

*Shunt boxes were moved from the rear of the vehicle bulkhead to the middle seat back from 1978, and now had a single ammeter incorporated into the shunt box, rather than the two on the dashboard. (Author's collection)*

underneath the vehicle floor. The reason for this is not known, and it does seem a very strange place to put it, being so exposed to the elements.

In early 1978 a major change was to take place that would affect FFR Half-Tons, i.e. the introduction of the new Clansman radio system. This was to gradually replace the earlier Larkspur system, and meant new types of cable assemblies, connectors, and co-axial wing stowage provision. As the old Larkspur FFR items were not compatible with the new Clansman system, a vehicle modification kit was issued, so that early vehicles could be brought up to date. Most early Larkspur type FFR vehicles, which survived into the 1980s, were converted.

Those vehicles which were stationed permanently in Northern Ireland were not normally fitted with radio stations so they were not affected. Other vehicles not affected, of course,

*Opposite: Series 3 GS in use as a garrison patrol vehicle. It has the tailgate removed for easier ingress/ exiting. (Author's collection)*

were those used only for garrison general transport roles.

Battery boxes changed, from September 1979, to include quick release catches and different battery clamps which facilitated servicing.

The last Half-Tons built for British service, in late 1984, were 24 volt but not FFR (more on these later in the chapter). It was difficult to tell from the outside that these were 24 volt, of course, since they did not have the FFR fittings, i.e. the radio table or the co-axial aerial leads for the wings or the rear bulkhead. For a description of the FFR system, see Chapter 1.

## Series 3 Variants

### British Variants

There were the two basic types, the 12 volt General Service (GS), used as a personnel carrier and general transport vehicle, and the 24 volt Fitted For Radio (FFR). The latter had provision for charging additional batteries from the vehicle system, which could then be used to power radio stations or other applications needing a 24 volt independent power supply.

All early vehicles were built as soft tops, and almost certainly all the later ones as well. However, fairly large numbers were converted to hard tops as a unit modification by all three Services, with both left and right hand drive versions. In 1976 Land Rover made the Half-Ton available with the 2286cc diesel engine, most of which were used by the Netherlands and Denmark. The British armed forces stayed with the petrol engine.

*Series 3 FFR with a patrol. Mounted on the wing is a Larkspur aerial tuning unit. (Courtesy Imperial War Museum)*

### FFR Variants

FFR vehicles were fitted with an extremely varied range of equipment. Radio systems included the Larkspur system, of course, and later the Clansman integrated system, which was to replace about 11 different Larkspur vehicle radio sets with just 3 different Clansman radio sets. Components of the Ptarmigan digital communications secure systems were also used from the early 1980s, and were compatible with both Larkspur and Clansman systems. Ptarmigan was

17 HF 64

SIGNAL
SCHOOL

***Opposite top: A very typical FFR fitted with Clansman radios. (Author's collection)***

***Opposite bottom: An FFR vehicle being used as a Public Announcement vehicle. (Courtesy Clive Elliott)***

designed for use within NATO.

**PADS (Position and Azimuth Determining System)**

Artillery weapon systems today are often extremely accurate. This is because both the target position and the position of the weapon laid on that target, are known accurately. To use PADS, the carrying vehicle was positioned next to a survey point, which was known to be correct. The co-ordinates were entered into the PADS, via a control panel and, as the vehicle moved off, the system's inertial navigation system plotted the movement and bearing change of the carrying vehicle. A hour after the initial move off, the PADS could give the position to within ten metres for both Eastings and Northings, and to an accuracy of one mil for azimuth. The data could then be used for navigation, or put into Field Artillery Computer

***Early RAF Series 3 window hardtop with split tailgate, which was quite common on RAF vehicles. It is seen here before the later practice of adding the yellow body stripes was introduced. (Courtesy Ken Porter)***

***The most common type of hard top. (Author's collection)***

Equipment (FACE) for artillery gun control, for instance. Produced in the 1980s by Ferranti, PADS was housed in a container measuring 460cm x 450cm x 250cm and weighing about 35kg. The Royal Artillery were major users of this equipment. A typical carrying vehicle would have been an FFR hard top Half-Ton (just one example of a non-radio application).

**Hard Tops**

All Rover 1 vehicles were ordered as soft tops, and almost certainly all Series 3 vehicles as well. I have found no evidence that any were actually ordered as hard tops. However, a production design for a modified hard top was completed in 1969. It was the basic item but with special closing panels to suit the narrower body. The first Half-Ton fitted with a hard top was Rover 1 chassis number 23600006, and a kit was made available for conversions. Since the hard tops were mostly the standard ones, as fitted to normal 88in wheelbase vehicles, this meant that they were not flush with the body sides because, of course, the Half-Ton was 4in narrower than the normal 88in wheelbase vehicles, and did not have the barrelled body sides.

When a hard top was fitted, a full rear door normally replaced the tailgate, though some had hinged upper halves, retaining the normal lower tailgate (these were mostly seen on RAF vehicles). Most were plain hard tops, though there were some window hard tops and a limited number of tropical roofed ones. The most unusual variant was the civilian pattern Station Wagon hard tops.

Hard tops were fitted for several reasons:

1) Security: it would then be possible to lock up a vehicle's contents, whether useful spares or tools, or just other military kit, or when a vehicle, particularly an FFR, had some sensitive equipment.

2) Warmth: many winterised Half-Tons were hard tops with additional insulation material fitted to the inner sides and roof.

3). It was easier to make a hard top light-proof by, for instance, plating or painting over the windows, thus avoiding giving the vehicle's position away to a potential enemy.

***Station Wagon hard top. Note that the windows are overpainted. (Author's collection)***

**Line Layer**
These were almost identical to the Rover 1 vehicles (see Chapter 1). Later Series 3 vehicles were also used in this role but by this time improvements in communications in general had made landline obsolete. The last conversions were withdrawn in the late 1980s.

**Parachute Regiment**
The Parachute Regiment used the Half-Ton (including the Rover 1) in comparatively large numbers since they had to rely on small light vehicles due to the weight carrying limitations of aircraft. The less weight the better.

One method of delivering vehicles to the Drop Zone (DZ) was to airdrop them by parachute on a Medium Stressed Platform (MSP). This was a system which used a special shock absorbing pallet, which could take two Half-Tons at a time. Self inflating air bags within the platform took much of the impact stress, though the loaded vehicles still took a lot of punishment. This was countered by precise rigging with wooden packing pieces. The windscreen and door tops were removed and packed in foam packing, the lights were taped up and the vehicles were securely lashed and chained down. Two MSPs could be carried in one Hercules aircraft.

**Parachute Regiment Reconnaissance Vehicles**
One of the more interesting adaptations was for reconnaissance by forward elements of each Battalion. These FFR vehicles were modified by fitting a pintle mount in the load bed at the rear of the vehicle for a 7.62mm General Purpose Machine Gun (GPMG). The tailgate was removed and a fold down platform giving 360 degrees (6400 mils) field of fire was fitted in its place. When folded up, this also doubled as

***A REME vehicle displays a very unusual hard top. (Author's collection)***

an extra shelf for kit stowage. Stowage was very important, since at least four men and their personnel kit would be carried, and extra stowage provision was provided by adding an XPM basket on the bonnet. The doors were removed, and a jerrycan holder was positioned on each seatbox. Grab rails were fitted using the tilt frame sockets in the body, and simple fold down shelves were bolted on each side for Bergans and other kit.

The spare wheel was normally bolted onto the side footwell, sometimes one on each side. No radio operators' seats were fitted, but a mounting for a Clansman manpack was. A small number of vehicles were additionally armed with bumper-mounted smoke dischargers.

A later modification was to fit a cut down Land Rover One Tonne roll cage, to provide protection against roll over accidents. These vehicles have now all been replaced by Land Rover 90s. All the conversions were carried out by REME (Royal Electrical Mechanical Engineers) craftsmen at unit workshops.

**RAF Use**

The RAF used Half-Tons, including a small number of Rover 1s, for various roles, including general cargo use, and as personnel carriers. Other uses were as glider tugs at gliding schools, basic fire tenders, motive power for towed trolley equipment, and even aircraft tugs. They were also used as 'Follow me' signed vehicles for aircraft guidance to dispersal areas.

Most Land Rovers on airfields were equipped with orange rotating beacons on safety grounds. Many RAF Half-Tons had hard tops fitted, and some in very cold regions were fitted with the large C.J. Williams heaters. The RAF Police and RAF Regiment both used the winterised hard tops.

The RAF Regiment also used VPK-fitted vehicles in Northern Ireland in the 1970s (see Chapter 3).

One very extraordinary variant used by the RAF was the conversion to a full tracked vehicle. James Cuthbertson Ltd. did the work. At least two were built and were believed to have been used for bomb disposal on aircraft bombing ranges. These were based on early Series 3 vehicles, and the conversions were carried out in August 1973. The vehicles were in service until at least 1980. It seems

***Series 3 Line layer. (Courtesy Clive Elliott)***

official approval for this conversion was not granted by either Land Rover or MVEE.

Some vehicles used by the RAF were 24 volt 90 amp, but not Fitted For Radio. These were presumably to power non-radio applications needing a 24 volt supply, and some were certainly classed as Helicopter Starting vehicles. The last British Half-Ton contract was indeed for 24 volt 90 amp vehicles, and most (if not all) of these went to various units in the RAF (including at least two to the Red Arrows). These went into service in early 1985.

**Royal Navy Use**

The Royal Navy used Half-Tons in some

***Para reconnaissance vehicle in Wales. Note the stowage basket on the bonnet. The GPMG mount is not fitted. (Courtesy Dunsfold Collection)***

***Parachute Regiment reconnaissance Half-Ton. These FFR vehicles were modified by fitting a pintle mount at the rear of the vehicle in the load bed, for a 7.62mm General Purpose Machine Gun (GPMG) and were modified by 10 Airborne Workshops REME. (Courtesy REME Museum)***

***Land Rover 90 on an MSP. This type of vehicle replaced the Para Reconnaissance Lightweight. (Author's collection)***

***One very extraordinary variant used by the RAF was this Cuthbertson conversion to a full tracked vehicle. Based on early Series 3 vehicles, at least two were built and were believed to have been used for bomb disposal on aerial ranges. (Courtesy British Motoring Industry Heritage Trust)***

***Interior view which clearly shows the extra windows in the canvas for greater visibility around aircraft at RAF gliding schools. (Courtesy Richard Caney)***

numbers, including the first Rover 1s to go into service, though most were used by the Royal Marines. One unusual variant was that used as a helicopter service platform. These vehicles had a frame with a platform fixed over the sides, to provide an elevated working area. The Royal Marines, of course, were among the first units to use the Wombat BAT recoilless rifle, mounted on Half-Tons.

***This hard top served with the Red Arrows, and is in their colours. It is seen here at dealer PB Blanchards after being sold. (Courtesy Peter Blanchard)***

**Winterised Half-Tons**

The standard factory-fitted Smiths heater in the Half-Ton was not considered effective in extreme conditions. Therefore, for vehicles on the ORBAT of units that deployed to Norway, or other very cold areas, a unit modification (actually fitted to both Rover 1s and Series 3s) was used to combat the extremes of cold weather. The modification consisted of a large heater made by the British firm C.J Williams, mounted in the centre of the seat base, taking up

***A 24 volt 90 amp vehicle in bright yellow for use as a glider school vehicle at RAF Lyneham in 1992. (Courtesy Clive Elliott)***

the middle seat. On FFR vehicles the battery box was removed and the two batteries were relocated into lockers in the rear wheelarches, one on each side. This meant that the tool locker at the nearside wheelarch was removed, and a new tool locker fitted under the bonnet as on later vehicles. GS vehicles had the vehicle battery relocated in the rear load bed.

The heater had four large hoses, branching off, directed onto the windscreen, and into the rear of the vehicle. Most vehicles had hard tops fitted and an insulation material,

Series 3, of 29 Commando Regiment, Royal Artillery, stripped down with a GPMG on exercise in Sardinia in 1988. The hessian covers on the lights are to prevent light reflection. (Courtesy Royal Marines Museum)

Royal Marine GS vehicle, Northern Ireland 1977. (Courtesy Royal Marines Museum)

***Royal Marine Series 3s. Note the vehicle with the "RN" number. (Courtesy Royal Marines Museum)***

***Interior view of a winterised vehicle showing the heater valve and inter-vehicle battery slave start. (Author's collection)***

called 'Plasterzote', was liberally applied throughout (rubber floor mats were also used). Window blinds and a radiator blind were fitted, and sometimes a vehicle to vehicle battery slave starter socket in the passenger footwell. Winterised vehicles often had studded tyres fitted, and some came with mud flaps.

The conversions were not done by Land Rover but were undertaken as a unit modification and were used by all three British services. Not all vehicles had all of the above variations fitted.

C.J. Williams, the manufacturer of the conversion kit, was taken over by Pro-Tech Precision Ltd in 1992.

48 HG 69

48
HG69

***A Winterised Series 3 wading. The heater pipes in the cab are clearly visible in this view. (Courtesy Royal Marines Museum)***

***Opposite: Winterised vehicle in 1992. (Author's collection)***

***One interesting variant was this Gloster Saro conversion for use in the Falklands (see also Chapter 4). (Courtesy Crown Copyright/MoD)***

*In 1997 the MoD decided to dispose of the entire Series 3 fleet. This vehicle, which belonged to the Gurkas, is seen in December 1997. (Author's collection)*

*23 HF 82 of the Honourable Artillery Company, towing a 25 pounder gun at the Lord Mayor's Show, London, 1997. (Courtesy PM Photography)*

***05 KD 63 was within the last Half-Ton contract and served in Hong Kong with the RAF and later with a TA REME unit. It is a 24 volt 90 amp vehicle and is seen here in 1997, just before being sold out of service. (Author's collection)***

***The Land Rover 90 was the vehicle which gradually replaced the Half-Ton. This one is a GS soft top. (Author's Collection)***

***Another view of a Land Rover 90. This one is an FFR hardtop and belonged to an RA unit. It was photographed in 1991. (Author's Collection)***

# 3 AT WAR

The Half-Ton was, of course, built as a purely military machine, and has consequently seen service in various conflicts and peace keeping operations throughout the world. Although primarily used by the British armed forces, of course, the armed services of various other countries have also used the Half-Ton. The Half-Ton was used during the Gulf war between Iran and Iraq; in the former Yugoslavia with various United Nations (UN) countries and several combatants; and also in the Sudanese civil war, for example. Of these conflicts, one stands out as the longest and most involved for the Half-Ton, this being 'the Troubles', in Northern Ireland.

## Northern Ireland

### Introduction

When the British Army became involved in helping the civil power in 1969, many people believed that the situation would not last very long. The Army, in fact, was initially unprepared for a role in internal security in this type of situation. One of the biggest problems was to provide protection for troops who, for the most part, were using 'soft

***Parachute Regiment Rover 1 with the UN in Cyprus in the early 1970s. (Courtesy Guy Pelham)***

***Dutch vehicle in use as a training aid for UN service in the former Yugoslavia 1993. (Courtesy Sectie Militaire Geschiedenis Landmachtaf)***

skin' vehicles in the form of Bedford trucks and Land Rovers, sometimes with doors, tilts and tailgates removed to allow rapid exiting and better all round visibility.

Early on in the conflict, Land Rovers (Rovers 8, 9, 10 and 11), including Half-Tons, were fitted with expanded metal plate mesh (XPM) guards, to the front and side windows, the front could be raised by a wire and pulley when needed. Wire cutters were often fitted (see photographs), in the same way as to Jeeps and similar vehicles in World War Two, to prevent injuries from wire strung across the road (it being common practice for troops to stand up in the back, looking around). Sandbags were sometimes placed on the floor to deflect mine blasts, although they were still vulnerable to missiles, petrol bombs, shrapnel, and, of course, bullets.

Armoured vehicles available at the time were Alvis Saracens, Humber Pigs (some of which had been bought back from dealers by the MoD, after being disposed of!). There were also armoured Commers and Humber Pigs requisitioned from the Royal Ulster Constabulary (RUC). In some respects these vehicles were not really suited for the type of service that they were being used for, and they were expensive to run and labour intensive to maintain.

In early 1971, a number of 'soft skin' vehicles were attacked with Claymore type mines, with devastating results. It was quickly realised that something needed to be done. The Commander Land Forces NI, Major General Farrar-Hockley instructed

HQ REME to find a counter-measure against these mines, which could be readily fitted to standard GS vehicles, and to Land Rovers in particular.

**Vehicle Protection Kit**

The REME second in command in the province, Major Reg Pearce, was at that time carrying out ballistic trials on some Glass Reinforced Plastic (GRP) sheets. When it was decided to test these sheets against blast and shrapnel attacks, they appeared effective. He then designed a Vehicle Protection Kit (VPK) out of GRP to cover a Land Rover 1/4 Ton. REME approached the Royal Navy (RN), which had experience of using GRP to make conning towers and other parts for use on submarines. The RN Dock Yard, Chatham, agreed to make up one kit from Pearce's drawings to suit a Land Rover 1/4 Ton. This was completed in about a week and flown to NI where it was fitted to a vehicle. In front of senior military and RUC officers, the GRP kit was subjected to attack from a Thompson SMG, nail and Claymore bomb attack. The trial proved to be a success and approval was given to begin in-service manufacture in bulk.

**Production and Characteristics of GRP Armour**

The RN began production of the kits at the Royal Naval dockyards at Chatham, Portsmouth and Devonport in the early part of 1971. At Chatham, where Nelson's 'Victory' was built, work went on from 7.30am to 8pm seven days a week, and even the submarine programme was suspended.

The Royal Air Force at St. Athan also produced the kits, but it seems that, initially, most of the VPKs were built and fitted at the REME Workshop at Donnington, Shropshire. Later, most vehicles were fitted with the VPKs at 46 Command Workshop (later 46 Northern Ireland Workshop) at Kinnegar and Ballykelly NI. The VPKs were made up of preformed parts, ready for fitting. The major components numbered about 20 to 30 pieces depending upon who made the kit. Some kits, for example, used several small pieces for a component instead of one large piece. The Half-Ton kit weighed approximately 560lb (254kg).

The GRP was made by using glass matting, made up of flat bands (called rovings) of fibres about 8mm wide interwoven at right angles. This new type of armour was produced by gel coating a female mould and putting between 6 and 8 layers of matting down, each with a sparingly applied coat of resin between (GKN at Telford were involved with production methods and tooling for the moulds). The female and male halves of the mould were joined and

*REME mechanics carry out repairs to a Half-Ton during the Falklands War. (Courtesy REME Museum)*

*Vehicles in the early part of the Northern Ireland conflict had no protection. Here a very early Rover 1 is seen with a patrol. (Courtesy Royal Marines Museum)*

SP6
72 FG 87

***Rover 1 of 45 Commando, Royal Marines, with a Ferret armoured car in 1970. Of note are the Jerry can holders on the wings. (Courtesy Royal Marines Museum)***

*Rover 1, of 3 Infantry Brigade, with a VPK fitted, no roof hatch (but a young Land Rover fan). Note the wire cutter attached to the bumper, and factory fitted Dunlop 'Trackgrip' tyres. (Courtesy Imperial War Museum)*

***A late Rover 1 in Green/Black. The doors have been removed to enable quick debussing. (Courtesy Imperial War Museum)***

the whole unit was pressed and heated until cured. The armour finished up between 6 and 8mm thick. After release it was trimmed, holes were drilled, and a part number and code of origin were stencilled onto the finished parts. Sometimes a numbered diagram of the components was moulded on the inside of the bonnet piece. The kits were then packed with all of the required parts and fittings ready for use.

It was found during ballistic tests that a hard dense panel of GRP would shatter when hit by a round, showering particles of fibres and resin. Production panels, therefore, had small air pockets between the layers of matting and each strand of fibres. As a round began to penetrate, each layer would break, absorbing and dissipating the energy layer by layer.

It was found that the resin used in the construction of the kits rotted footwear, so old army boots were acquired for use by the personnel making up the kits!

The armour has often been referred to as Makrolon, which is, strictly speaking, incorrect. Makrolon is, in fact, a trade name for the polycarbonate plastic developed by the Bayer Chemical Company and used for riot shields, helmet visors and the like. On the actual VPKs, Makrolon was used on the rear door windows and on the cut outs for the rear lights (when driving with the rear doors open, it was still possible for those in following vehicles to see the rear lights). Makrolon would sometimes be used instead of XPM on the side windows, and was sometimes fitted inside vehicles over the windscreen, as a shatter shield.

The GRP armour was almost blast-proof, fire-resistant and, to certain low velocity ammunition, bullet-proof (***e.g.*** 9mm, .45in ACP at 25m). With higher velocity rounds, it would considerably slow the penetrating round. In some situations GRP armour was better than conventional armour, because it would not contain an explosion. Instead, an explosion would blow off the panels resulting in less chance of harm to the occupants.

## Variants

Many different vehicle types were fitted with VPKs, but these are outside the scope of this book. Early vehicles included the Rovers 8 and 9. Large numbers of Half-Tons were fitted with VPKs, both 'Trucks 1/2 Ton 4x4 Rover 1' and '1/2 Ton Utility 4x4 Rover Series 3'. These included GS and FFR vehicles. By the end of 1972, 752 VPKs had been made for the Half-Ton. Early vehicles did not have roof hatches, but these would soon become standard. These were used for observation and to provide top cover when on patrol. There were two types, and sizes:

1). Integral moulded roof and opening.

2). Roof with cut out opening and bolted on separate moulded hatch opening. There were also two sizes. This was not a problem on the 3/4 Ton, but

***Amongst the last of the Rover 1s, 00 FL 64, a GS, has had most VPK armour removed to provide better all round visibility. The doors and tailgate have also been removed to enable quick exiting. The rear floor, wheelarches, bonnet and belly plate armour have been retained. The spare wheel is mounted on the bumper. (Courtesy Imperial War Museum)***

on the 1/2 Ton, the larger type would result in the hatch cover, when open, resting on top of the spare wheel if it were mounted on the roof, as it usually was. Because of the windscreen XPM, it was very unusual to leave the spare in the normal position on the bonnet. Spare wheels were usually mounted on the roof, though some were mounted on the front bumper, or carried in the rear. Very occasionally the spare was mounted outside on the rear passenger side.

Another variant was in the fitting of folding Makrolon side screens around the roof hatches, though this was rare on Half-Tons, most being seen on 3/4 Ton Rovers.

Most vehicles were fitted with mesh windscreen and light guards. Nearly all Land Rovers were fitted with wire cutters. Interestingly, these were not included in the actual VPKs when delivered, and no mention of them is made in any of the fitting instructions (or of Makrolon roof side screens). Presumably the wire cutters were manufactured by REME metalsmiths at Workshop level. There were two types:

1). Bolted on to the windscreen pivot point and through the roof and left hand stiffener panel above the side window.

2). Bolted through the side body GRP panel (behind the left hand seat) using an internal steel plate as support. These were made from substantial angle iron. Alternatively one could be bolted to the front bumper.

The early VPKs differed in some respects from later kits for the Series 3.

***A Claribel radar equipped Series 3 FFR leads two Humber Pigs, whilst members of the RUC look on. (Courtesy Imperial War Museum)***

The main differences being:

1). Some early kits had rear windows, in addition to those in the doors.

2). Early VPKs were more complex to fit, having more panels. Some even required additional cutting before fitting was possible. Most vehicles fitted with VPKs were Series 3s. The kits for GS and FFR vehicles were identical.

Some vehicles were fitted with rear steps, whilst others had the NATO tow hook removed to make entry/exiting easier.

It was fairly common practice to see vehicles with extra armour, which was not part of the standard kit, including panels on seat bases, or extra panels bolted on the rear sides, on top of the standard panel (usually where someone would be sitting).

All three services used VPK Half-Tons in Northern Ireland. The main user, however, was the Army, including the newly-formed Ulster Defence Regiment (UDR). Although the UDR mostly used 3/4 Ton Land Rovers, when a UDR unit took over a regular Army TAOR (tactical area of responsibility), it would also take over the vehicles that were used by the outgoing unit (in patrolling the secure segments of Belfast city centre, for example). In July 1992 the UDR was merged with the Royal Irish Rangers to become the Royal Irish Regiment.

The RAF Regiment used Series 3 Half-Tons to patrol around Aldergrove Airport and the surrounding area. It used its vehicles with GRP armour, but retained the tilt (rolled forward), with tailgate down and an additional hoop to stop the occupants falling out! These vehicles had orange beacons as standard. Later, the Series 3 Half-Tons were replaced by Series 3 3/4 Ton vehicles with standard style GRP armour.

***Series 3 with a newly fitted Northern Ireland Vehicle Protection Kit. It was not usual practice to leave the spare wheel on the bonnet (Courtesy REME Museum)***

The Royal Marines often used Half-Tons, and it was not unknown for vehicles to have the side and/or rear doors removed, to make exiting easier (though, of course, there was no protection). Door panels, when delivered, often had flaps over the door handle holes, and these were often removed to make it easier to get into the vehicle in a hurry. On later kits these were deleted altogether.

The Parachute Regiment (and others) often used stripped down vehicles, the only armour present, therefore, was that on the rear floor, wheelarches, bonnet, belly plate and bulkhead. The reason for this was to give better all round visibility and make getting out of the vehicle easier. It was fairly common for the Parachute Regiment to use stripped down vehicles.

On several occasions during the conflict, vehicles were attacked with mines. As a countermeasure, designed to protect the crew from serious injury from the use of culvert land mines, a major modification was carried out which involved fitting substantial roll cages and inertia reel seatbelts to some vehicles. The delivery programme for this modification commenced in January 1977. Most VPK Land Rovers, however, retained the normal tilt frame.

At the end of their service life some vehicles were fitted with 'Joker' jammers to disrupt signals for improvised explosive devices (IEDs). A mounting for the aerials was fitted forward of the roof hatch, so the spare tyre was often mounted on the passenger side.

The Half-Ton's size was ideal for patrolling built-up areas as it could accommodate the minimum 'brick' of

*A stripped down Series 3 FFR, of the Royal Artillery, at the scene of an explosion at the BBC building, Ormeau Avenue, Belfast. (Courtesy Imperial War Museum)*

*South Armagh, an RAF Westland Wessex HC2, flies in with an unarmoured and partially stripped Half-Ton, to assist with a search team. In the foreground, a solider of the UDR provides cover. It became necessary to use helicopters for many operations in South Armagh, rather than road vehicles, due to the IRA's increasing use of landmines. Half-Tons were ideal for the role. (Courtesy Imperial War Museum)*

12 FM 96

***Undoubtedly the lightest Half-Tons ever, were these vehicles used by EOD and specialist units for operations in areas where road transport was considered to be too dangerous. They were stripped of all unnecessary components to reduce the height profile and weight for airborne operations. This gave a tactical advantage, since airlifting could be accomplished quickly. Note that even the bulkhead has been cut down, and minimum instruments are fitted. This one is seen at REME 46 Command Workshop, Kinnegar. (Courtesy Imperial War Museum)***

four men. It's not surprising, then, that the Half-Ton saw service in Northern Ireland from the early days of 'the Troubles' right up until the Land Rover VPKs were withdrawn from service in 1994.

**Claribel**

Some Series 3 Half-Ton vehicles were fitted with ground surveillance Claribel radar sets, developed by Microwave and Electronic Systems Limited as a sniper location set, giving an all round detection capability both day and night. A clock type indicator was provided to show the direction of fire. Recognition features were small pods, which looked like ventilators on the vehicle sides and on the front and rear.

**Explosive Ordnance Disposal Use**

One very unusual use of the Half-Ton in Ulster, in a true airportable role, was to carry 'wheelbarrow' robots, which were used to deal remotely with IEDs. These vehicles were completely stripped of all the body panels, including the floor and seatbox, to save weight. Even the unnecessary chassis crossmembers were cut off. A simple shorter exhaust was fitted, along with a smaller battery and radiator. The bulkhead was cut down, leaving the absolute minimum to support the steering wheel, while the instrument panel and most instruments were removed. A simple cover was placed over the engine to keep off the rain. The two 10-gallon fuel tanks were removed and replaced with a 5-gallon one. A single seat was provided for the driver and, to complete the vehicle, a ramp was provided on top of the chassis for the wheelbarrow. These vehicles did not normally display numberplates, and they would be inserted into the operational area by helicopter. This was necessary when the route to the site of the IED could be compromised and mined.

Half-Tons were also used with trailers equipped with 'Lilliput' jamming equipment, utilised to protect troops by suppressing radio controlled IEDs.

The Half-Ton in Ulster was used for general transport roles and the odd specialist role as just mentioned. Other bolt-on gadgets were public

*Here we have a front view of the Half-Ton wheelbarrow carrier. (Courtesy Imperial War Museum)*

*Wheel barrow carrier in use by 321 Explosive Ordnance unit Company, RAOC on operations in South Armagh in 1981. This photograph was supplied by Paul Wharton, a former bomb disposal officer who recalled that "The Land rover (code named Gobbler) was worth its weight in gold whenever there was a need to drag heavy stuff about - which was often, and of course it was air portable by helicopter. (Courtesy Paul Wharton)*

address systems, and various types of spotlight. Radios were not usually fitted, as the patrol commander and 2/IC would normally carry a pocketphone, or Cougar radio.

**Modifications for Fitting GRP VPKs**

The major advantage of the VPK was that no special tools were required to fit the kits, standard hand tools only were needed. A vehicle could be fitted with a complete kit in about 32 to 35 man-hours. Basically, the VPK was just bolted to the outside of the vehicle. When a vehicle was no longer required with the VPK, it was a simple job to remove it, leaving only a few holes to show that it had ever been fitted. These would be filled with plastic plugs.

The only major modification required was the fitting of large cylindrical rubber pads (called Aeon springs), that sat between the axle and chassis (the bump stops having been removed), with a shoe plate welded on top of the affected axle. They were originally meant to be fitted only on the front of the Half-Ton, but often seem to have been put on all axles.

Vehicles were painted in accordance with theatre of operation instructions. This meant early vehicles were painted in deep bronze green, later in NATO green and, contrary to popular belief, disruptive NATO green and black (see Chapter 4). During the late 1980s, 'Spafax' plastic anti-shatter mirrors (type TM2) were often fitted. Vehicles sometimes had Goodyear road tyres fitted, rather than Goodyear 'Xtra Grips'.

*An RAF Westland Wessex lifts a Half-Ton wheelbarrow carrier. In the background are the cranes of the Harland and Wolfe shipyard. (Courtesy Imperial War Museum)*

***A Series 3 VPK at Masonic Camp, Londonderry city center, with an early confidential telephone number stencilled on the sides. (Courtesy Imperial War Museum)***

**Use of Confidential Telephone Numbers**

Every unit in NI used to hand out courtesy cards to people that they met on patrol. These would contain a telephone number which people could use if they wished to pass on any information. The telephone numbers varied depending on the area. For instance, Belfast was 652155, and Londonderry 262340. These local numbers were advertised in newspapers and sometimes stencilled onto the sides of vehicles (particularly Land Rovers). In the late 1970s, the RUC introduced the Robophone answering machine, since it was found that people preferred to give information anonymously. The Robophone was a large, complicated and expensive unit and was a forerunner of today's modern small telephone answering machines. Because they were so expensive, they could only be hired from the Robophone Company. To avoid the, by now, multitude of different telephone numbers, a uniform freephone telephone number was introduced in April 1988. It then became common practice (and still is), to stencil the number on the body sides in yellow or red (fuel filler cap colours). The new number being 'CONFIDENTIAL TELEPHONE 0800 666999'. This was done by the user and was not always very neat. The old phone numbers were still in use at the time of writing.

**Summary**

The Northern Ireland glass reinforced plastic Vehicle Protection Kits were a clever innovation to solve a problem which needed a rapid answer. They were cheap (compared to normal armoured vehicles), and more importantly, they were a quick solution to the protection of soldiers and their vehicles. Although they may have been crudely made and often fitted in a hurry, the kits did provide genuine protection from attack and

***Series 3 with the later 0800 666999 confidential telephone number displayed. (Courtesy Clive Elliott)***

***Driver training in a Rover 1 VPK. Goodyear road tyres are fitted. Note the interior Makrolon sliding screen. This gave protection from flying glass and other missiles. The headlights of both vehicles are also protected by Makrolon sheets. (Courtesy Imperial War Museum)***

*A REME mechanic working on a Half-Ton in Northern Ireland. (Courtesy REME Museum)*

saw widespread use, particularly on Land Rovers. As weapons on the other side improved, VPKs became less effective against attack. The solution was the Land Rover HV (High Velocity) VPK (Piglet), and later, the Land Rover APV and CAV (Snatch). These, however, came at a much higher cost. The last Land Rover VPK vehicles were withdrawn from use in 1994. Out of the many hundreds of Land Rover Half-Tons fitted with VPKs only one is known to survive with a VPK fitted.

***The Half-Ton VPK was replaced in the early 1990s by versions of the 110, including the 110 Glover Webb APV, as seen here ... (Courtesy Tom Finlay)***

***... and the 110 Courtaulds CAV. (Courtesy Tom Finlay)***

# 4 BRITISH COLOUR SCHEMES & EQUIPMENT

## Army and Royal Marines Vehicle Schemes

Early vehicles were delivered in High Gloss Deep Bronze Green, which was the normal finish. Unpainted parts, such as the bumper and windscreen and body cappings, were galvanised to prevent rusting. In 1969, it was decided that units which had a front line role should paint their vehicles in a scheme appropriate for the theatre of operation. This standard scheme was a basic mid-olive green, which was over-painted in disruptive pattern black. For most of the 1970s, however, vehicles were still delivered in Deep Bronze Green. The end of the 1970s saw the introduction of infra-red reflective (IRR) paint finishes, which had the effect of reducing a vehicle's infra-red signature to IR detectors. Most vehicles were then delivered in this scheme of NATO IRR Green, to which units could then apply IRR black on top. This was the standard finish until the end of production. The disruptive finish was extremely varied due to the fact that it was applied by units, or at workshops, but the general idea was to break up the outline of the vehicle by applying roughly two thirds green to one third black. EOD vehicles had red wings added. Defence Fire Service vehicles were sometimes red.

Canvas tilts were sometimes over-painted too with special canvas paint, usually just adding disruptive black or green or, sometimes, both colours. Vehicles used in Norway were usually painted in White, often with IRR Green or Black disruptive patches. UN vehicles were normally white all over. Light Stone colour was applied to vehicles used in desert areas, although some odd schemes appeared during the 1991 Gulf War, including sand and pink patterns, and sand and green.

Another variation was that applied to vehicles used in Cyprus and BATUS, which were normally painted in stone with green disruptive patches.

Some vehicles were actually repainted in the original Deep Bronze Green for ceremonial occasions. Examples of this included the vehicles belonging to the Honourable Artillery Company in London, which were used as gun tractors for Second World War 25 pounder field guns - a role for which they were never designed. These vehicles replaced earlier Rover 8s in January 1988 and were withdrawn in late 1998.

## RAF Vehicle Schemes

Early vehicles were delivered in RAF Blue Grey. In 1973 some were delivered in Green but most were still RAF Blue Grey up until the late 1970s, when vehicles were delivered in NATO IRR Green, to which units could then apply IRR Black, if desired. This was the standard finish until the end of production. Again, Light Stone colour was applied to vehicles used in desert areas.

From the late 1970s onwards, on safety grounds, yellow stripes were often added to vehicles. This was so that they could be clearly seen from the air. Some vehicles used by glider schools were painted yellow all over (often on the inside as well), to be even more visible from the air.

5

Loading a Wombat onto a Rover 1 in Malta. The vehicle is painted sand and green, including the inside. (Courtesy Royal Marines Museum)

A Rover 1. Army and Royal Marines vehicles were painted Bronze Green. This shot was taken during jungle training. (Courtesy Royal Marines Museum)

*NATO green was the standard finish from the mid 1970s. Of note is the RAF type tilt normally seen on glider school vehicles. In fact, this is an Army vehicle. (Author's collection)*

*Individual units could then add disruptive black. (Courtesy Imperial War Museum)*

***White for Norway. (Courtesy Royal Marines Museum)***

## Markings

Markings common to all British vehicles are the stencils for Petrol, Oils and Lubricants (POL). Examples of these were found on the axles, the steering boxes and the gearbox: OEP 220 for gear oil, OMD 75 (later OMD 80) for engine oil, AL 11 for windscreen washer fluid, AL 39 for anti freeze, and OX 8 for brake and clutch fluid.

For airlifting purposes, chalk markings were often stencilled onto the doors or bonnet. Weight markings, normally chalked onto the doors, provided the AUW (all up weight), RAW (rear axle weight) and FAW (front axle weight), a practice which is still in use today. Tyre pressures were normally stenciled on the wheelarches. Other stencils used included radio call signs, often on doors, along with tactical signs such as broken circles and triangles. Unit badges were sometimes displayed on doors, bonnets, and on the rear of vehicles. Vehicles stationed overseas usually carried the Union Flag sticker, front and rear, in various positions. Metal bridge plates were carried on the front of the vehicle. The Half-Ton classification was 2, so this was often displayed on the bridge plate, which was yellow (at least on Rover 1s and early Series 3s). Later vehicles often had the bridge plates the same as the vehicle colour scheme or, from August 1977, in grey.

It was normal practice to paint the rear axle differential (or at least part of it) white, for the convoy light to have

***Gulf war markings on this sand vehicle. (Courtesy REME Museum)***

something bright to shine onto. NATO trailer socket cover caps were often painted blue for FFR, and yellow for GS vehicles.

## Tyres

All British vehicles were fitted on the production line with 5.00 x 16 commercial wheel rims (FV607330), which were well-base type, fitted with 6.50 x 16 tubed tyres. Divided wheel rims were not used on the Rover 1, even though most Rover 8s and some very early Rover 10s at the time had 4.50 x 16 divided wheel rims (FV84919).

On early Rover 1 vehicles 6.50 x 16 Dunlop 'Trakgrips' were the factory-fitted specification. These tended to be replaced by Goodyear bargrips or 6.50 x 16 Goodyear Hi Miler Xtra Grips when in service use, which became the standard fitment. Winterised vehicles often had studded tyres.

Other tyres which were often fitted included road-biased Goodyear tyres, particularly in Northern Ireland and on RAF vehicles. Vehicles used in the 1991 Gulf War sometimes had sand tyres fitted, such as Michelin 'XSF'. RAF Half-Tons also had 6.50 x 16 Michelin 'XCLs' fitted. It was not unknown for Half-Tons to have 7.50 x 16 tyres, but this was not common. At the end of their working lives in the late 1990s it was common to see vehicles with odd, locally purchased tyres, where units could not get the standard 6.50 x 16 Goodyear 'Xtra Grips', which were no

***United Nations vehicles were also white, Cyprus 1974. (Courtesy Royal Marines Museum)***

11 FM 99

*Even some very late vehicles were in Bronze Green for ceremonial occasions. All of the HAC vehicles were transferred from the Royal Green Jackets in 1988, rebuilt, and were used until 1998 for ceremonial occasions. (Author's collection)*

*This vehicle was amongst the first RAF Series 3s, in factory finish, in RAF Blue Grey, with Dunlop Trakgrips fitted. (Courtesy Ken Porter)*

***RAF glider school vehicle in yellow. (Courtesy Richard Caney)***

longer in production. A small number of Army vehicles were modified by Gloster Saro, and fitted with 151/2in wide low profile tyres. These were for use in the Falkland Islands to give greater cross country performance.

***This 1974 RAF vehicle displays the common addition from the late 1970's of yellow stripes to its bodywork. (Courtesy Simon Sage)***

***27 GJ 73 of the Military Police. The crosses on the doors are exercise markings. (Courtesy Imperial War Museum)***

KEYSTONE
COPS
MILITARY POLICE
27 GJ 73

TP 30
22A
TP30
CHALK
FAW
RAW
AUW
TP 25

43A

*Opposite top: This view shows the typical British stencil markings, tyre pressures, chalk numbers, and radio call sign on the door. (Author's collection)*

*Opposite bottom: 43 A is a radio call sign prominently displayed on a door. (Author's collection)*

*This hard top was used as a display vehicle by the Royal Irish Regiment, and has its badge on the doors. (Author's collection)*

*Opposite top: A Marine kneeling in front of a Rover 1 fitted with Goodyear Hi Miler 'Xtra Grip' tyres, Ulster 1978. (Courtesy Royal Marines Museum)*

*Opposite botton: A REME mechanic changes a bargrip tyre on a Rover 1. (Courtesy Imperial War Museum)*

*32 FK 05 is really MXC 682H (with a false numberplate) a Rover 1 demonstrator fitted with Dunlop 'Trakgrip' tyres. (Courtesy Dunsfold Collection)*

93KA66

93
KA66

*Opposite: A small number of vehicles were converted in the mid-1980s for use in the Falklands, the work being done by Gloster Saro Ltd. at Hucclecote. The modifications included large 15½ " tyres, 8 psi front, 12 psi rear, flared wheelarches, exhaust run out branch and a substantial sump guard and new bumper. (Courtesy Gloster Saro)*

*View of the sump guard. (Courtesy Gloster Saro)*

*A new bumper was designed to carry the spare tyre. (Courtesy Gloster Saro)*

# 5 FOREIGN SERVICE

## Introduction

Land Rover exported its vehicles world wide, of course, and military sales of the Half-Ton were to be no exception. The first overseas customers for the Series 3 were Belgium and Libya, which took some in 1972/3. The main foreign users were to be Libya, Saudi Arabia and The Netherlands. The other countries listed below had relatively smaller numbers.

However, in countries with restrictive import regulations, heavy import duties, or other limits to free trade, the policy was to supply vehicle parts, from which assembly plants abroad could build up vehicles. Often only major components were supplied by Solihull, with many other components being supplied by the destination country. A good example of this was with the two foreign versions of the Half-Ton, that of Spain, with Santana, which had a high percentage of Spanish components. Later, the Iranian company Morrattab made its own unlicensed version of the Spanish Half-Ton (using parts from Spain, in fact), though it should be said that these vehicles were not designed to be stripped for airporting, and were more of a styling exercise.

No Series IIA Half-Tons were purchased by foreign armed forces, all being used by the British Services. Nevertheless, considerable numbers of Series 3s were used by the military authorities of the following countries: Algeria (Morrattab and possibly Santana), Belgium, Belize, Brunei, Croatia (ex-Dutch), Denmark, Egypt (Miltar), Guyana, Hong Kong, Indonesia, Iran (Morattab), Jamaica, Libya, Morocco (Miltar), The Netherlands, Oman, Portugal, Saudi Arabia, Slovenia (ex-Dutch), Spain (Miltar), Sudan, and Uganda.

## Denmark

The Danish Armed Forces mostly used the 2286cc diesel engine Half-Ton (though they did use some petrol models which were delivered in 1974). The Danish diesel trials vehicle (chassis number 95401408) was converted from petrol to diesel in June 1978. After the trials it went to their stocks. Delivery of the Danish diesel vehicles commenced in 1979.

One interesting variant was that fitted with the American BGM-71A TOW (Tube-launched Optically-tracked, Wire-guided) anti-tank system. This weapon was developed by Hughes Aircraft Ltd. in 1965, originally to replace the American M40 106mm recoilless rifle, which was also put to use on the Half-Ton (see Marshall of Cambridge M40 A1, below). TOW came into service in 1970, and first saw operational service with helicopters in 1972 in the Vietnam War. TOW

***Opposite top: Danish Series 3 Half-Ton of an artillery unit at Sjaelsmark Barracks, March 1998. (Courtesy Martin Pagh)***

***Camouflaged vehicle with netting and foliage, photographed at the Royal Danish Lifeguards' Hoevelte Barracks. (Courtesy Martin Pagh)***

48.472
48.472

52.623
52 623

***Opposite top: A rear view of a Series 3 TOW vehicle, minus the firing post. Photographed in April 1999. (Courtesy Martin Pagh)***

***Opposite bottom: A Series 3 with the American BGM-71A TOW (Tube-launched Optically-tracked, Wire-guided) anti-tank system. Photographed in August 1999. (Courtesy Martin Pagh)***

was a successful weapon system, which has been mounted on various platforms, including Jeeps (indeed, the Danish Army had used the M151 Jeep). The calibre of the TOW was 6 inches, utilising a shaped charge with an effective tactical range of 65 to 3750 metres. The weapon system was still in use with the Danish Army in the year 2000, though the 60 (TOW) Land Rover vehicles have now been replaced by the American (TOW) HMMWV. There was also a support vehicle that carried extra ammunition and a radio. Some stripped down vehicles, without a windscreen, were also used in a reconnaissance role.

Detail differences on Danish vehicles included side indicator lights on the wings, a night-driving 'notek' style convoy light on the bumper, and a small roof rack was usually fitted. Some had one piece side hinged tailgates. Danish vehicles had 7.50 x 16 tyres.

Other standard vehicles were used by the Danish for UN use in Cyprus with the United Nations Forces in Cyprus (UNFICYP). These were British Service vehicles on lease.

**The Netherlands**

The Netherlands armed forces took delivery of both petrol and diesel powered vehicles from August 1976 onwards. The majority, however, were 24 volt, 60 amp, 2286cc diesel engined Half-Tons. A small number (three or possibly four) were used for trials in late 1972, the trials contract being ordered in September 1972. The trials vehicles had standard British indicator and sidelight arrangements,

***KZ 13 12 is one of the Dutch trials vehicles delivered in 1972. (Courtesy Sectie Militaire Geschiedenis Landmachtaf)***

***Interior view of a trial vehicle. (Author's collection)***

with the addition of a 'notek' night convoy light on each wing. There were a number of other detail changes, plus the addition of Dutch pattern lights. The trials vehicles were given non-standard Dutch chassis numbers ending with 'X'.

Project Engineer, Bob Seager recalls, "Trials took many months, and were painful in the extreme. Driving was done by conscript soldiers, who found out that if they damaged a vehicle, they could loaf around until it was fixed. The novel ways they found to put a motor off the road was amazing. I don't remember how many vehicles were supplied, but it was a sizeable number."

The later Dutch production vehicles differed in quite a number of respects from the normal Series 3, the biggest change of course being that of the diesel engine, as opposed to the normal 2286cc petrol one. Detail differences were considerable. These included a battery isolator and a NATO style convoy light on a rubber flap. The latter was detachable and had its own stowage position between the front seats next to the first aid box. The passenger side door was fitted with a stowage pocket. There were also changes to the lighting arrangements, and all light units were changed to the Dutch pattern. Many instruments were changed too: the light switch was new, as was the slave starter socket in the passenger footwell, the indicator switch was now mounted on the

***KM 23 18, of the Dutch Marines, carrying an M40 A1 106mm recoilless rifle. (Courtesy Royal Marines Museum)***

bulkhead, and a map light was fitted as standard. Vehicles had additional amber reflectors on the body sides and white ones next to the headlights. A pair of night driving lights was fitted onto the top of each wing, along with a pair of combined indicator and side lights. A single blackout brakelight was also used.

The standard gun clips were replaced with Dutch pattern ones. A transparent coloured convoy cover could be fixed over the passenger's side headlight using the loops provided for that purpose. On the opposite side, the national flag was normally applied next to the headlight. The national marking 'NL' was often applied on a black band on the bonnet, usually along with unit markings. An 'S' on the bonnet denoted that the vehicle was electrically suppressed to prevent interference with radios. The radio table was a much smaller and simpler affair than the British version. The Dutch fitted many different types of tyres to their vehicles, all of which were left hand drive of course.

Most of the vehicles were used by the Army (National Service) and, on the disbandment of National Service, most of the Dutch vehicles were withdrawn from service in 1992/3. Some of the last surviving Army vehicles served with the United Nations in Cyprus and the former Yugoslavia. Royal Netherlands Marines vehicles served with the UN in Cambodia.

***KX 22 76 leaves Havelte Barracks. Note the convoy light cover in place.***
***(Courtesy Sectie Militaire Geschiedenis Landmachtaf)***

The arm of the services to which a vehicle belonged was identifiable by the registration letters: KL, KN to KZ were Army (KL = Koninklijke Landmarcht); the Royal Netherlands Marines vehicles had the letters KM (Koninklijke Marine).

**Marshall of Cambridge M40 A1 Recoilless Rifle Carrier**

In around November 1976, Marshall of Cambridge (Engineering) Ltd. designed a modification of the Half-Ton to carry the American designed M40 A1 106mm recoilless rifle which had come into service in 1965. This was fitted using the M79 mounting, the actual weapons being built under license by Pakistan Machine Tool Factory Ltd. These vehicles entered service with the Saudi National Guard in 1977, at least 50 being delivered. The modification changes included, 7.50 x 16 tyres, blast shields on the bonnet and wings (which doubled as stowage provision for a pick and shovel), rear seats with drop down seat backs to give an arc of fire of 180 degrees forward. The spare wheel was mounted on the passenger side, or on the bonnet with a large blast shield, and the windscreen was split to make way for the barrel. A barrel clamp was mounted on top of the bulkhead. The ranging gun was an M8C 0.5in spotting rifle. Other known users were the Sudan and Oman, and

***Rear view of a communications vehicle in the field. (Courtesy Sectie Militaire Geschiedenis Landmachtaf)***

at least 100 vehicles were built. It is believed that Kuwaiti units during the 1991 Gulf War used some of the Saudi vehicles. By 1988, Marshalls had designed a replacement for the Half-Ton M40 A1 carrier, on the Land Rover 90 chassis.

Bob Seager recalls, "We did an exercise for an African country with a Russian recoilless rifle. This was a 75mm weapon, and a lot shorter than the 106mm. We borrowed a gun this time from Royal Ordnance, who have a wonderful collection of weapons from all over the world. We could not work out a method of firing forward without causing major blast damage, but the order fell through before we got to the trial stage."

**Morrattab**

In the late 1980s, the Iranian company Morrattab began building an unlicensed version of the Half-Ton using CKD kits from the Spanish company Santana. This came about because of the 1973 Arab/Israeli 'Yom Kippur War', after which Iran barred British vehicles from being imported into the country. This allowed the Spanish company Santana to begin exporting its vehicles to Iran. After some time, however, the bulk of the componentry of the finished vehicles was locally supplied.

The Iranian vehicles were somewhat different from the Spanish vehicles. They had the headlights within the radiator panel, for example, as on the early Series IIA, and the spare tyres were fixed onto the footwell panels or the rear body sides. The Iranian vehicles also differed quite considerably from the normal Land Rover Half-Ton. For example, they were fitted with barrelled type doors rather than the more usual flat type. The wings on the Iranian vehicles were of a different design. They also had an external filler neck for the fuel tank, and were fitted with a curved bonnet.

A version fitted with a 106mm recoilless rifle was also available, some of which were supplied to Algeria. 7.50 x 16 tyres were fitted as standard.

It should be noted, however, that airportability was not a consideration in these designs.

**Santana**

The Spanish company, Metalurgica de Santa Ana SA, more commonly known by its trade name Santana, based in Linares, produced its own version of the Half-Ton for the Spanish military. Known as the Santana 88 Militar, and available from 1970, these were not actually designed to

***KX 30 58. The S on the bonnet denotes that the vehicle is suppressed to prevent interference with radios. It is seen here at a military driving school at Venlo in 1979. (Courtesy Sectie Militaire Geschiedenis Landmachtaf)***

***Close up view of the lighting arrangements on a Dutch vehicle. The 'Notek' light on top of the wing is for tactical night driving. (Author's collection)***

be airportable as such, but were, instead, just basic utility vehicles. They were actually a lot heavier than their British counterparts. All were 24 volt, and were fitted with the 2286cc petrol engine. The basic version was the soft top, but some hard top versions were produced as well. Other variants included one fitted with an M40 A1 106mm recoilless rifle carrier (which was similar to the Marshall of Cambridge (Engineering) Ltd. design), and a Milan anti-tank missile launcher. The Militar had a very distinctive front, in that small rectangular lights were fitted into the higher cut-down wings, which had a normal style rounded-type bonnet. It also sported a plastic grill instead of the normal metal mesh one. This displayed the Land Rover badge with Santana underneath in smaller letters.

These were sold to other armed forces, including those of Egypt, Morocco, and very possibly Algeria, and around 3500 were made.

A civilian version called the 88 Ligero (Spanish for 88 Lightweight) was made available in 1980. Most had freewheeling hubs and a black tilt. Late vehicles had front disc brakes and an anti roll bar on the front axle.

***Around November 1976, Marshall of Cambridge (Engineering) Ltd., designed a modification of the Half-Ton to carry the American designed M40 A1 106mm recoilless rifle. Many of these vehicles were used by Saudi Arabia. The lower picture shows the rear view after the conversion. (Courtesy Marshall of Cambridge Ltd.)***

Iranian version of the Half-Ton seen at a trade fair in 1988. (Courtesy Simon Thompson)

Santana Ligero brochure. (Courtesy Santana)

The Spanish company Metalurgica de Santa Ana SA, or, as it was more commonly known, Santana, produced its own version of the Half-Ton for the Spanish military. Known as the Santana 88 Militar, these were not actually designed to be airportable as such, but were intended as basic utility vehicles. (Courtesy Santana)

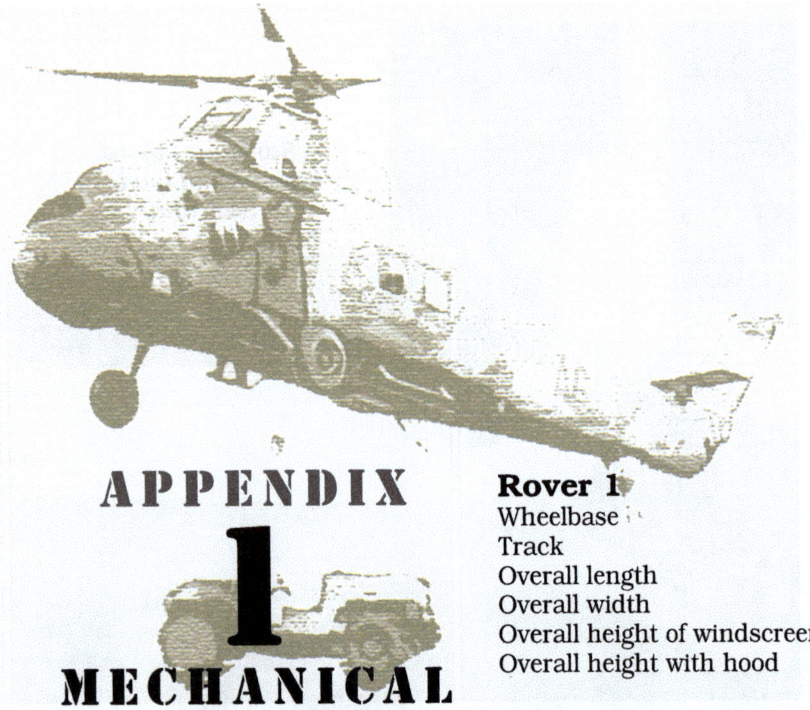

# APPENDIX 1 MECHANICAL DATA

| **Rover 1** | ***Imperial*** | ***Metric*** |
|---|---|---|
| Wheelbase | 88in | 2.23m |
| Track | 51.5in | 1.31m |
| Overall length | 144in | 3.65m |
| Overall width | 60in | 1.52m |
| Overall height of windscreen | 67in | 1.70m |
| Overall height with hood | 77in | 1.95m |
| Loading area | 48 x 55.5in | 1.21 x 1.40m |
| Ground clearance | 8.5in | 0.21m |
| Turning circle | 42ft | 12.80m |
| Unladen weight | 3210lb | 1456kg |
| (stripped) | 2660lb | 1206.5kg |
| Gross vehicle weight | 4450lb | 2018.5kg |

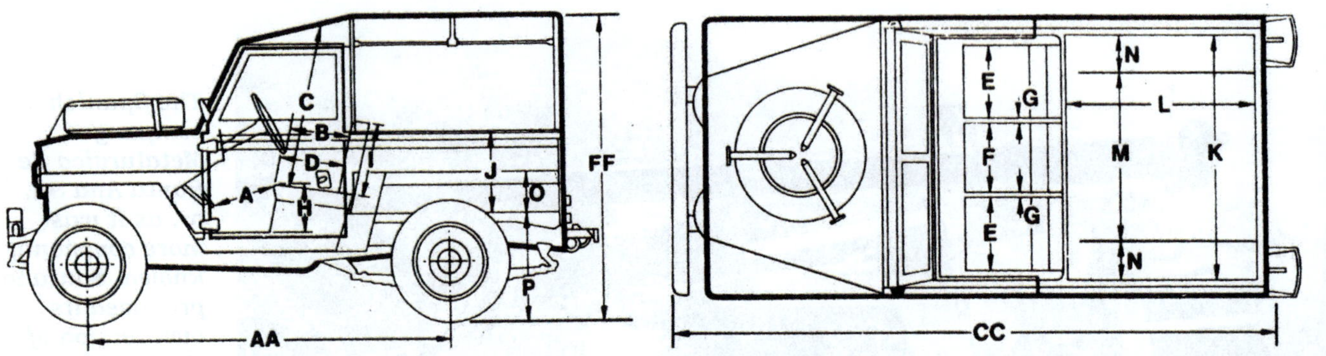


| | | ***Metres*** | ***Inches*** |
|---|---|---|---|
| AA | Wheelbase | 2.23 | 88.00 |
| BB | Track | 1.31 | 51.50 |
| CC | Overall length | 3.65 | 144.00 |
| DD | Overall width | 1.52 | 80.00 |
| EE | Overall height of windscreen | 1.70 | 67.00 |
| FF | Overall height with hood | 1.95 | 77.00 |
| A | Front cushion to accelerator pedal | 0.44 | 17.50 |
| B | Front squab to steering wheel | 0.36 | 14.25 |
| C | Headroom, front seat (uncompressed) | 1.05 | 41.50 |
| D | Front to rear of front cushion | 0.43 | 17.12 |
| E | Width of front cushion | 0.45 | 18.00 |
| F | Width of front centre cushion | 0.45 | 18.00 |
| G | Width between front seats | 0.02 | 1.00 |
| H | Top of front cushion to floor | 0.35 | 14.00 |
| I | Front squab height | 0.46 | 18.00 |
| J | Height of body sides | 0.50 | 20.00 |
| K | Width of body interior | 1.48 | 55.75 |
| L | Length of body interior | 1.14 | 46.25 |
| M | Interior body width between wheel boxes | 0.91 | 36.00 |
| N | Width of wheel boxes | 0.28 | 11.60 |
| O | Height of wheel boxes | 0.20 | 8.12 |
| P | Platform height (unladen) | 0.71 | 28.00 |

**Engine**
Type: 2.286 litre, 4 cylinder petrol, max power: 77bhp @ 4250rpm, max torque, 124lb.ft at 1500rpm.

**Transmission**

| | | |
|---|---|---|
| Main gearbox ratios: | ***Top*** | ***Direct*** |
| | 3rd | 1.512:1 |
| | 2nd | 2.22:1 |
| | 1st | 3.6:1 |
| | Rev | 3.0:1 |
| Transferbox ratios: | High | 1.148:1 |
| | Low | 2.4:1 |
| Axle ratio front and rear: | 4.7:1 | |

**Equipment**
Tyre size: Five alternatives - 6.00in x 16in, 6.50in x 16in, 7.00in x 16in, 7.50in x 16in, 8.20in x 15in (sand tyres)
Wheel rim size: 5.00in F x 16in well-base.
Electrical system: 12 volt dc, 24 volt ac.

**Performance**
Approach angle: 49 degrees (58 degrees in stripped down form).
Departure angle: 36 degrees (38 degrees in stripped down form).
Payload: (road and cross-country): 10cwt (508kg).
Maximum speed: 65mph (105kph).
Gross power/weight ratio (laden): 40bhp/ton.
Maximum tractive effort: 4000lb (1800kg laden).

## Land Rover Military Classification

The various basic military British types were classed, at least until the Series 3 was introduced, as follows:
Rover Mk 1 was the 80in Series 1 with the 1595cc engine.
Rover Mk 2 was the 80in Series 1 with the 1997cc engine.
Rover Mk 3 was the 86in Series 1 with the 1997cc engine.
Rover Mk 4 was the 107in/109in Series 1 with the 1997cc engine.
Rover Mk 5 was the Series 1 88in with the 1997cc engine.
Rover Mk 6 was the 88in Series II.
Rover Mk 7 was the 109in Series II.
Rover 8 was the 88in Series IIA.
Rover 9 was the 109in Series IIA.
Rover 10 was the 88in Series IIA from 1967.
Rover 11 was the 109in Series IIA from 1967.
Suffix /1 indicates that strengthened differential and axle shafts were fitted to the rear. (Applied to Rover 8 and 9 only).
Suffix /2 indicates that neither the strengthened differential or axle shafts were fitted to the rear. (Applied to Rover 8 and 9 only).
Confusingly, the 88in Series IIA Half-Ton was initially classed as Rover Mk 1.

## Chassis Numbering

The Half-Tons had their own chassis numbering system, which differed from other Land Rover types.
Series IIA, 88in. All were petrol 2286cc.

| | ***Starting at*** |
|---|---|
| RHD | 23600001 to 23601893 |
| LHD | 23900001 to 23901096 |
| Series 111, 88in | |
| Diesel Export LHD | 89500001 to 89501909 |
| RHD | 95100001 to 95105805 |
| Export RHD | 95200001 to 95100102 |
| CKD RHD | 95300001 (none built) |

*Close up of a typical data plate, found on the inside of a Rover 1 vehicle. (Author's collection)*

*Close up of a typical data plate, found on the inside of a Series 3 vehicle. (Author's collection)*

| | |
|---|---|
| Export LHD | 95400001 to 95404518 (includes British forces vehicles) |
| CKD LHD | 95500001 (none built) |

The system was to change in 1979, when the Half-Ton was allocated a 17-digit VIN (Vehicle Identification Number) prefix letter code as below. This meant:
SA = British Leyland, L= Land Rover, LB = Series 3.

| | |
|---|---|
| Petrol 2286cc vehicles were in the range: | RHD SALLBBAH1AA plus 6 digits |
| | LHD SALLBBAH2AA plus 6 digits |
| Diesel 2286cc vehicles were in the range: | LHD SALLBBAG2AA plus 6 digits |

Chassis numbers can be found stamped on the front right-hand spring shackle bracket, also on an aluminium data plate fixed to the seat box, and to the bulkhead, which would also have the vehicle contract number. On later Series 3 vehicles, with VIN numbers, the data plate was often located inside the engine bay, fixed onto the bulkhead.

## Nomenclature

The Half-Ton has over the years, confusingly been given various official designations, for example, the Rover 1 alone was classed as:

Truck, General Service Lightweight FFR (Rover Mk 1, 1/4 Ton 4x4) (preproduction).
Truck, General Service, FFR, 1/2 Ton, 4x4 Rover Mk 1.
Truck, General Service, FFR, 1/2 Ton, 4x4 Rover 1.
Truck, Utility, FFR, 1/2 Ton, 4x4 Rover 1.
Truck, General Service Lightweight (Rover Mk 1, 1/4 Ton 4x4) (preproduction).
Truck, General Service, Cargo, 1/2 Ton, 4x4 Rover Mk 1.
Truck, General Service, 1/2 Ton, 4x4 Rover Mk 1.
Truck, General Service, 1/2 Ton, 4x4 Rover 1.
Truck, Utility, GS, 1/2 Ton, 4x4 Rover 1.
Truck, Utility, 1/2 Ton, 4x4 Rover 1.

***Notes on codes: All vehicles used by the British Armed Services are given an Asset Code. For 'soft skin' vehicles the code is normally prefixed by B for 'B vehicles'. The letter prefix usually only appears on paperwork not actually on the vehicle. The codes were introduced in about 1960, and the system is a little complicated. However, Land Rovers (88in wheelbase) were allocated codes from 1150-**** to 1674-****. The first four digits indicating***

***a particular type, for example, Truck, GS, 1/2 Ton, Rover 1 and Series 3 were allocated 1620. The last four numbers gave more information, for instance, 1620-0772 is Truck General Service, 1/2 Ton, 4x4, Rover 1 (RHD). 1620-5778 is Truck, Utility, 1/2 Ton, 4x4, Rover Series 3 (LHD).***

**Truck 1/2 Ton FFR and GS Asset Vehicle Codes**

| Code | Type | Remarks |
|---|---|---|
| 1616 0778 | Truck, Utility, 1/2 Ton, 4x4 Rover Series 3 | (RHD) |
| | With Full Track Conversion | (Cuthbertson) |
| 1618-0783 | Truck, Utility, 1/2 Ton, 4x4, 24 volt 90 amp, Rover, Series 3 | (RHD) |
| 1618-5783 | Truck, Utility, 1/2 Ton, 4x4, 24 volt 90 amp, Rover, Series 3 | (LHD) |
| 1620-0772 | Truck, General Service, 1/2 Ton, 4x4, Rover 1 | (RHD) |
| 1620-0778 | Truck, Utility, 1/2 Ton, 4x4 Rover Series 3 | (RHD) |
| 1620-5772 | Truck, General Service, 1/2 Ton, 4x4, Rover 1 | (LHD) |
| 1620-5778 | Truck, Utility, 1/2 Ton, 4x4 Rover Series 3 | (LHD) |
| 1625-0778 | Truck, Utility, FFR, 1/2 Ton, Rover Series 3 | (RHD) |
| 1625-0772 | Truck, General Service, FFR, 1/2 Ton, 4x4, Rover 1 | (RHD) |
| 1625-5772 | Truck, General Service, FFR, 1/2 Ton, 4x4, Rover 1 | (LHD) |
| 1625-5778 | Truck, Utility, FFR, 1/2 Ton, 4x4, Rover Series 3 | (LHD) |
| 1670-0772 | Truck, General Service, 1/2 Ton, 4x4, Rover 1 | (RHD)(RAF/RN) |
| 1670-5772 | Truck, General Service, 1/2 Ton, 4x4, Rover 1 | (LHD)(RAF/RN) |
| 1674-0772 | Truck, General Service, FFR, 1/2 Ton, 4x4, Rover 1 | (RHD)(RAF/RN) |

***Notes***

***1). In March 1972 the term 'General Service' in the description title of Rover 1s was deleted, in favour of 'Utility'.***

***2). Half-Tons modified to Glider Recovery were recoded 1614-****, but this would not be displayed on the vehicle, as it would keep the original data plate.***

***3). Half-Tons coded 1618-****, were originally for Helicopter Starting.***

***4). Half-Tons modified with the winterised kit were recoded 1619-****, 1624-**** or 1626***, but this would not be displayed on the vehicle, as it would keep the original data plate.***

***5). Half-Tons modified with Wombat were recoded 1645-****, but this would not be displayed on the vehicle, as it would keep the original data plate.***

***6). The 1670-**** and 1674-**** codes were recoded to 1620-**** and 1625-****.***

**NATO Stock Numbers (NSN)**

| NSN | Code | Type |
|---|---|---|
| 2320-99-806-8679 | 1620-5772 | Truck, Utility, GS, LHD, Rover 1 |
| 2320-99-808-1494 | 1620-0772 | Truck, Utility, GS, RHD, Rover 1 |
| 2320-99-808-1971 | 1625-0772 | Truck, Utility, FFR, RHD, Rover 1 |
| 2320-99-893-2659 | 1625-5772 | Truck, Utility, FFR, LHD, Rover 1 |
| 2320-99-893-2845 | 1620-0778 | Truck, Utility, GS, RHD, Series 3 |
| 2320-99-893-2846 | 1620-5778 | Truck, Utility, GS, LHD, Series 3 |
| 2320-99-893-2847 | 1625-0778 | Truck, Utility, FFR, RHD, Series 3 |
| 2320-99-893-2848 | 1625-5778 | Truck, Utility, FFR, LHD, Series 3 |
| 2320-99-893-2973 | 1618-0783 | Truck, Utility, 24 volt 90A, RHD, Series 3 |
| 2320-99-893-2974 | 1618-5783 | Truck, Utility, 24 volt 90A, LHD, Series 3 |
| 2320-99-893-6502 | 1624-0783 | Truck, Utility, 24 volt 90A, (W) RHD, Series 3 |
| 2320-99-893-6503 | 1624-5783 | Truck, Utility, 24 volt 90A, (W) LHD, Series 3 |
| 2320-99-893-6512 | 1619-0778 | Truck, Utility, GS, RHD, (W) Series 3 |
| 2320-99-893-6515 | 1619-5778 | Truck, Utility, GS, LHD, (W) Series 3 |
| 2320-99-893-6519 | 1626-0778 | Truck, Utility, FFR, RHD, (W) Series 3 |

## Test and Demonstrator Vehicles

The first prototype was built in 1965, when trials began at the FVRDE, this was not believed to have been registered. Another early prototype was 20 BT 90. This was sold off at Ruddington on 31 October 1976.

There were also the following LHD demonstrator vehicles, the first two built in 1967:

23900001, VXC 702F the first LHD vehicle, built 14 December 1967; 23900002, the second production LHD vehicle, built 22 December 1967, went to Rover Melbourne as a demonstrator.
23900003, built 28 August 1968, an FFR, was retained by Land Rover's Government Sales Department and became NXC 25H (and the first vehicle to be modified with headlights on the wings). It was displayed in 1970 at the FVRDE exhibition, along with one unregistered vehicle, 23900004, which went to Rover's Engineering Department.
The first RHD, production vehicle, an FFR, CXC 212G (chassis 23600001, once in the Dunsfold collection) was registered on 4 October 1968. This vehicle also carried the military registration 20 BT 91.
23600006, was retained by military sales and used as personnel transport, it was RAF Blue (and was the first vehicle to be modified to a hard top).
23600007 was retained by military sales, and was Bronze Green.
23600008 was retained by military sales, and was Bronze Green.
The first RHD Series 3, chassis number 95100001, was built 7 April 1972, and went to Land Rover's Engineering Department.
95400703 went to Land Rover's Engineering Department as GXC 966L.

## British MoD Half-Ton Contracts

**Contract WV5101 (Pre-production) July 1966 -**

| ***Registration numbers*** | ***Chassis no*** | ***Location & date of sale*** |
|---|---|---|
| 00 SP 13 became 21 BT 92 then 60 EP 78 | 24125521C | CER (PE) 20 Feb 1973 |
| 00 SP 14 became 21 BT 84 then 60 EP 79 | 24426934C | FVRDE unknown date |
| 00 SP 15 became 21 BT 85 | 24125945C | Ruddington 24 Aug 1973 |
| 00 SP 16 became 60 EP 81 then 21 BT 93 | 24427323C | Ruddington 4 Nov 1975 |
| 00 SP 17 became 21 BT 94 | 24126991C | FTM/Sales 23 Jan 1970 |
| 00 SP 18 became 21 BT 95 then 60 EP 80 | 24127158C | CER (PE) 20 Feb 1973 |

***1) The chassis numbers fall within standard Rover 8 batches from 1966, these were used in trials.***
***2) The military registration serials 50 EP 00 to 99 EP 99 were for ex-civilian registered vehicles, at military bases, under the control of Master General of Ordnance 1965/6.***
***3). Army registration 'BT' serials were transferred vehicles. 'SP' serials were for special projects.***

**Royal Air Force Contracts Rover 1 Half-Ton -**

| ***Contract*** | ***Date into service*** | ***Reg Range*** | ***Type*** | ***Census Code*** |
|---|---|---|---|---|
| WV8391 | 1969 | 71 AA 17 to 71 AA 48 | FFR | 1625-0772 |
| WV8391 | 1969 | 99 AA 76 to 99 AA 97 | FFR | 1625-0772 |
| WV8551 | 1969 | 13 AA 73 to 14 AA 16 | GS | 1620-0772 |
| WV8551 | 1969 | 99 AA 42 to 99 AA 75 | GS | 1620-0772 |

**Army and Royal Marines Contracts Rover 1 Half-Ton -**

| ***Contract*** | ***Date into service*** | ***Reg Range*** | ***Type*** | ***Census Code*** |
|---|---|---|---|---|
| WV7477* | 1969 | 71 FG 97 to 72 FG 88 | GS | 1620-0772 |
| WV7478 | 1969 | 33 FG 35 to 43 FG 34 | GS | 1620-0772 |
| WV7850 | 1969 | 59 FG 61 to 60 FG 16 | FFR | 1625-0772 |
| WV8459 | 1969 | 30 FH 49 to 30 FH 52 | FFR | 1625-0772 |
| WV8679 | 1969/70 | 53 FH 54 to 55 FH 40 | GS LHD | 1620-5772 |
| WV9753* | 1971 | 53 FJ 12 to 53 FJ 49 | FFR | 1625-0772 |
| WV10193 | 1971 | 26 FK 88 to 28 FK 39 | GS | 1620-0772 |
| WV10193 | 1971 | 28 FK 40 to 31 FK 99 | GS LHD | 1620-5772 |
| WV10318 | 1971/2 | 57 FK 11 to 60 FK 28 | FFR LHD | 1625-5772 |
| WV10318 | 1971/2 | 60 FK 29 to 62 FK 28 | FFR | 1625-0772 |
| WV10366 | 1972 | 64 FK 79 to 65 FK 78 | GS | 1620-0772 |
| WV10366 | 1972 | 65 FK 79 to 67 FK 28 | GS LHD | 1620-5772 |

***Contract WV9753 was for a limited number of Rover 1 FFR vehicles, the only ones with"FJ" numbers. (Courtesy Royal Marines Museum)***

| *(Continued ...)* **Contract** | **Date into service** | **Reg Range** | **Type** | **Census Code** |
|---|---|---|---|---|
| WV10552* | 1972 | 00 FL 62 to 00 FL 86 | GS | 1620-0772 |
| WV10551* | 1972 | 00 FL 87 to 01 FL 14 | FFR | 1625-0772 |

***Nominally Royal Navy contracts, however, vehicles from these were often used by Army units, and are in the Army registration series. RN Rover 1 contracts were WV7835, WV9322, WV9383 and WV10274, which had 'RN' registration numbers.***

**RAF Contracts Series 3 Half-Ton -**

| Contract No | Date into service | Registration range | Type | Census Code |
|---|---|---|---|---|
| WV10828 | 1972 | 53 AM 52 to 55 AM 29 | GS | 1620-0778 |
| WV10828 | 1972/3 | 55 AM 30 to 55 AM 59 | GS LHD | 1620-5778 |
| WV10828 | 1972/3 | 55 AM 60 to 55 AM 80 | GS | 1620-0778 |
| WV11131 | 1973/4 | 59 AM 20 to 59 AM 94 | 24V 90A | 1618-0783 |
| WV11131 | 1974/4 | 59 AM 95 to 60 AM 00 | FFR | 1625-0778 |
| WV11131 | 1973/4 | 60 AM 01 to 60 AM 19 | 24V 90A LHD | 1618-5783 |
| WV11131 | 1973/4 | 60 AM 20 to 60 AM 28 | FFR LHD | 1625-5778 |
| WV11147 | 1974 | 61 AM 04 to 62 AM 64 | GS | 1620-0778 |
| WV11147 | 1974 | 62 AM 65 to 62 AM 99 | GS LHD | 1620-5778 |
| WV11430 | 1974/5 | 71 AM 29 to 71 AM 64 | 24V 90A | 1618-0783 |
| WV11430 | 1974/5 | 71 AM 65 to 71 AM 68 | FFR LHD | 1625-5778 |
| WV11439 | 1974/5 | 71 AM 69 to 72 AM 68 | GS | 1620-0778 |
| WV11439 | 1974/5 | 72 AM 69 to 72 AM 80 | GS LHD | 1620-5778 |
| WV11700 | 1975/6 | 75 AM 46 to 76 AM 40 | GS | 1620-0778 |
| WV11700 | 1975/6 | 76 AM 41 to 76 AM 45 | GS LHD | 1620-5778 |
| WV11701 | 1975/6 | 76 AM 50 to 76 AM 75 | 24V 90A | 1618-0783 |
| WV11701 | 1975/6 | 76 AM 76 | 24V 90A LHD | 1618-5783 |
| WV11872 | 1976/7 | 77 AM 20 to 77 AM 64 | GS | 1620-0778 |
| WV11872 | 1976/7 | 77 AM 65 to 77 AM 74 | GS LHD | 1620-5778 |
| FVE22A/24 | 1978 | 88 AM 13 | GS | 1620-0778 |
| FVE22A/22 | 1978 | 88 AM 14 to 88 AM 60 | GS | 1620-0778 |
| FVE22A/22 | 1978 | 88 AM 61 to 88 AM 86 | GS LHD | 1620-5778 |
| WV11874 | 1976/7 | 29 AJ 83 to 29 AJ 92 | GS | 1620-0778 |
| WV11874 | 1976/7 | 29 AJ 93 to 29 AJ 96 | 24V 90A LHD | 1618-5783 |
| FVE22A/24 | 1977/8 | 30 AJ 88 to 31 AJ 00 | 24V 90A | 1618-0783 |
| FVE22A/24 | 1977/8 | 31 AJ 01 to 31 AJ 11 | 24V 90A LHD | 1618-5783 |
| FVE22A/40 | 1977/8 | 31 AJ 90 to 32 AJ 64 | GS | 1620-0778 |
| FVE22A/40 | 1977/8 | 32 AJ 71 to 33 AJ 15 | GS LHD | 1620-5778 |
| FVE22A/94 | 1979 | 39 AJ 82 to 40 AJ 31 | GS | 1620-0778 |
| FVE22A/94 | 1979 | 40 AJ 32 to 40 AJ 52 | GS LHD | 1620-5778 |
| FVE22A/115/12 | 1980 | 43 AJ 25 to 43 AJ 27 | 24V 90A | 1618-0783 |
| FVE22A/115/15 | 1980 | 43 AJ 69 to 43 AJ 83 | GS LHD | 1620-5778 |
| FVE22A/115/16 | 1980 | 43 AJ 84 to 45 AJ 08 | GS | 1620-0778 |
| FVE22A/115/15 | 1980 | 47 AJ 08 to 47 AJ 16 | GS LHD | 1620-5778 |
| FVE22A/115/16 | 1980 | 47 AJ 17 to 47 AJ 70 | GS | 1620-0778 |
| FVE22A/115/16 | 1980 | 48 AJ 09 to 48 AJ 16 | GS | 1620-0778 |
| FVE22A/115/15 | 1980 | 49 AJ 15 to 49 AJ 16 | GS LHD | 1620-5778 |

***Note: Some vehicles were transferred to the Army; these were then given numbers in the BT range, for instance: 54 AM 44 to 46 BT 93, 59 AM 40 to 40 BT 81, 59 AM 58 to 40 BT 83.***

**Army Contracts Series 3 Half-Ton -**

| *Contract No* | *Date into Service* | *Registration range* | *Type* | *Census Code* |
|---|---|---|---|---|
| WV10787 | 1972/3 | 45 FL 36 to 51 FL 39 | GS | 1620-0778 |
| WV10787 | 1972/3 | 51 FL 40 to 54 FL 54 | GS/LHD | 1620-5778 |
| WV10775 | 1972/3 | 54 FL 55 to 56 FL 94 | FFR | 1625-0778 |
| WV10775 | 1972/3 | 56 FL 95 to 58 FL 77 | FFR/LHD | 1625-5778 |
| WV11139 | 1973/4 | 08 FM 57 to 17 FM 17 | FFR | 1625-0778 |
| WV11139 | 1973/4 | 17 FM 18 to 18 FM 77 | FFR/LHD | 1625-5778 |
| WV11140 | 1973/4 | 19 FM 20 to 26 FM 13 | GS | 1620-0778 |
| WV11140 | 1974 | 67 FM 75 to 69 FM 59 | GS | 1620-0778 |
| WV11140 | 1974 | 69 FM 60 to 70 FM 24 | GS/LHD | 1620-5778 |
| WV11139 | 1974 | 72 FM 90 to 75 FM 19 | FFR | 1625-0778 |
| WV11139 | 1974 | 75 FM 20 to 75 FM 39 | FFR/LHD | 1625-5778 |
| WV11404 | 1974/5 | 31 GB 08 to 33 GB 61 | FFR | 1625-0778 |
| WV11404 | 1974 | 33 GB 62 to 34 GB 11 | FFR/LHD | 1625-5778 |
| WV11581 | 1975 | 02 GF 39 to 03 GF 38 | GS | 1620-0778 |
| WV11581 | 1975 | 03 GF 39 to 04 GF 38 | GS/LHD | 1620-5778 |
| WV11706 | 1976 | 42 GF 78 to 45 GF 67 | FFR | 1625-0778 |
| WV11706 | 1976 | 45 GF 68 to 46 GF 34 | FFR LHD | 1625-5778 |
| WV11733 | 1975/6 | 52 GF 20 to 54 GF 57 | GS | 1620-0778 |
| WV11733 | 1976 | 54 GF 58 to 56 GF 57 | GS LHD | 1620-5778 |
| WV11733 | 1976 | 62 GF 31 to 62 GF 52 | GS LHD | 1620-5778 |
| WV11916 | 1977 | 26 GJ 94 to 27 GJ 53 | FFR | 1625-0778 |
| WV11916 | 1977 | 27 GJ 54 to 28 GJ 02 | FFR LHD | 1625-5778 |
| WV12086 | 1977 | 01 GN 62 to 01 GN 85 | FFR | 1625-0778 |
| WV12086 | 1977 | 01 GN 86 to 02 GN 11 | FFR LHD | 1625-5778 |
| FVE22A/39 | 1978 | 08 GT 70 to 09 GT 89 | GS | 1620-0778 |
| FVE22A/39 | 1978 | 09 GT 90 to 10 GT 19 | GS LHD | 1620-5778 |
| FVE22A/46 | 1978/9 | 26 GT 85 to 28 GT 43 | FFR LHD | 1625-5778 |
| FVE22A/70 | 1979 | 08 GX 70 to 10 GX 16 | GS | 1620-0778 |
| FVE22A/87/1 | 1979 | 17 HF 55 to 21 HF 06 | FFR | 1625-0778 |
| FVE22A/87/2 | 1979 | 21 HF 07 to 21 HF 46 | FFR LHD | 1625-5778 |
| FVE22A/87/3 | 1979 | 21 HF 47 to 24 HF 46 | GS | 1620-0778 |
| FVE22A/87/4 | 1979 | 24 HF 47 to 26 HF 63 | GS LHD | 1620-5778 |
| FVE22A/95/3 | 1980 | 15 HG 39 to 15 HG 81 | GS | 1620-0778 |
| FVE22A/95/4 | 1980 | 15 HG 82 to 16 HG 39 | GS LHD | 1620-5778 |
| FVE22A/95/5 | 1980 | 16 HG 40 to 16 HG 84 | FFR | 1625-0778 |
| FVE22A/95/6 | 1980 | 16 HG 85 to 17 HG 16 | FFR LHD | 1625-5778 |
| FVE22A/115/3 | 1980 | 45 HG 57 to 47 HG 36 | GS LHD | 1620-5778 |
| FVE22A/115/4 | 1980 | 47 HG 37 to 51 HG 26 | GS | 1620-0778 |
| FVE22A/115/5 | 1980/1 | 51 HG 27 to 52 HG 16 | FFR LHD | 1625-5778 |
| FVE22A/115/6 | 1980/1 | 52 HG 17 to 57 HG 39 | FFR | 1625-0778 |
| FVE22A/115/30 | 1981 | 05 HH 38 to 05 HH 76 | FFR | 1625-0778 |

**Tri-service Contracts Series 3 Half-Ton -**

| *Contract No* | *Date into Service* | *Registration range* | *Type* | *Census Code* |
|---|---|---|---|---|
| *Note from below* | *vehicles may be* | *either Army, RN or RAF* | | |
| FVE21B/229/1 | 1982 | 16 KA 92 to 17 KA 39 | GS | 1620-0778 |
| FVE21B229/4 | 1982 | 17 KA 49 | FFR | 1625-0778 |
| FVE21B/244/2 | 1983 | 83 KA 52 to 84 KA 38 | GS | 1620-0778 |
| FVE21B/244/3 | 1983 | 84 KA 39 to 85 KA 51 | GS LHD | 1620-5778 |
| FVE21B/244/7 | 1983 | 91 KA 96 to 93 KA 04 | GS LHD | 1620-5778 |
| FVE21B/244/8 | 1983 | 93 KA 05 to 93 KA 88* | GS | 1620-0778 |
| FVE21B/244/13 | 1983 | 22 KB 54 to 22 KB 79 | GS | 1620-0778 |

| *(Continued ...)* Contract | Date into service | Reg Range | Type | Census Code |
|---|---|---|---|---|
| FVE21B/244/17 | 1983 | 23 KB 07 to 23 KB 15 | GS | 1620-0778 |
| FVE21B/244/19 | 1983 | 23 KB 22 | 24V 90A | 1618-0783 |
| FVE21B/244/20 | 1983 | 23 KB 23 to 23 KB 41 | GS | 1620-0778 |
| FVE21B/244 | 1983 | 29 KB 72 to 30 KB 39 | FFR | 1625-0778 |
| FVE22A/225/1 | 1983 | 55 KB 86 to 58 KB 35 | GS | 1620-0778 |
| FVE22A/240/2 | 1984 | 84 KB 26 to 84 KB 47 | FFR LHD | 1625-5778 |
| FVE22A/240/3 | 1984 | 84 KB 48 to 85 KB 31 | GS | 1620-0778 |
| FVE22A/251/1 | 1984 | 40 KC 27 to 41 KC 32 | GS LHD | 1620-5778 |
| FVE22A/251/2 | 1984 | 41 KC 33 to 41 KC 82 | GS | 1620-0778 |
| FVE22A/251/6 | 1984 | 42 KC 44 to 44 KC 46 | FFR | 1625-0778 |
| FVE22A/251/7 | 1984 | 44 KC 47 to 44 KC 93 | FFR LHD | 1625-5778 |
| FVE22A/251/59 | 1985 | 05 KD 02 to 05 KD 11 | 24V 90A LHD | 1618-5783 |
| FVE22A/251/60 | 1985 | 05 KD 12 to 05 KD 65 | 24V 90A | 1618-0783 |

**** 93 KA 07 was cancelled***

***The above list may not be complete, particularly regarding later vehicles.***

## Berlin Garrison X Series Half-Tons -

As can be seen from the first batch (XB), the quantities were not great, and some, if not all, were not new when registered. Berlin being surrounded by the 'Red Menace' had no chance if hostilities broke out. The policy was to allocate old unimportant equipment to a force that would be overwhelmed in a very short time. All this is now history, of course, and the Berlin Garrison is no more. 'X' registrations denote that they were provided by the Berlin Senate.
All vehicles were LHD. There could possibly have been others.

| Date | Registration Range | Type | Census Code |
|---|---|---|---|
| Jan 1979 | 43 XB 85 to 43 XB 87 | FFR LHD | 1625-5778 |
| 1977 | 57 XB 36 to 57 XB 43 | FFR LHD | 1625-5778 |
| Jan 1977 | 57 XB 54 to 57 XB 65 | GS LHD | 1620-5778 |
| Jul 1973 | 04 XC 39 to 04 XC 95 | FFR LHD | 1625-5778 |
| Jan 1974 | 04 XC 96 to 04 XC 99 | GS LHD | 1620-5778 |
| 1974/75 | 05 XC 32 to 05 XC 60 | GS LHD | 1620-5778 |
| Jan 1975 | 05 XC 64 to 05 XC 73 | GS LHD | 1620-5778 |
| Jan 1973 | 21 XC 40 to 21 XC 59 | FFR LHD | 1625-5778 |

***Note: Unfortunately, it has proved impossible to find out any comprehensive information regarding the RN vehicles both Rover 1 and Series 3. The RN contracts being WV7835, WV9322, WV9383 and WV10274 (Rover 1) and WV11572, WV12040, FVE22A/8, FVE22A/9, FVE22A/18, FVE22A/25, FVE22A/45 and FVE22A/73 (Series 3), which had 'RN' registration numbers.***

# APPENDIX 2 BIBLIOGRAPHY & CLUBS

A parts microfiche for the Half-Ton was introduced by Land Rover for the dealer network, part number was RTC9968FA.
The following military publications were issued, copies of which may be hard to find. The RAF used similar publications and, in fact, in many instances the same.

**Army publications relating to Truck Utility, 1/2 Ton, 4x4, Rover 1**

| *Army Code* | *Publications* |
|---|---|
| 22178 | User Hand Book (issued August 1968) |
| 60344 | Servicing Schedule |
| 34171 | Complete Equipment Schedule (GS) |
| 34192 | Complete Equipment Schedule (FFR) |
| 60595 | Illustrated Parts Catalogue |

**EMERs Relating to Half-Tons**
The Army system supplied publications to maintain the Half-Ton fleet. These came under the Electrical and Mechanical Engineering Regulations, otherwise referred to as EMERs.
The block of EMERs (Wheeled Vehicles) relating to Rover 1 was Q 020/4 to Q 029/4 (the later Series 3 Half-Ton was EMER Q 020/13 to Q 029/13).
According to EMER index (1988) only three sections were published.

**EMER Q 020/4 Data Summary**
Issued 1 Nov 1968. Note: during March 1972, the term General Service (in description title) was deleted in favour of Utility.

**EMER Q 025/4 Waterproofing Instructions No. 1, (May 1969) 2, 3, and 4.**

**EMER Q 027/4 Modification Instructions**

| | |
|---|---|
| No. 1 | Not known. |
| No. 2 | Turn light switch wiring, brought up to date on chassis 2360100 Jan 1970. |
| No. 3 | Mounting of Wombat, March 1970. |
| No. 4 | Fitting of commercial heater/demister on contract WV8679 (only) and vehicles used in NW Europe. |
| No. 5 | Strengthening of seat bases to prevent spot weld failure, Sept 1974. |

**EMER Q 029/4 Miscellaneous Instructions**

| | |
|---|---|
| No. 1 | New designation of EMER, Q020/7 to Q020/4, Sept 1969. |
| No. 2 | Fitting stretcher kit, March 1971. |
| No. 3 | Replacement of unitary radio plug and sockets, Feb 1978. |

Many other modifications and miscellaneous instructions from the main block of EMERs Q 020 - Q 029 affect the Rover 1, but were also intended for the earlier and later vehicles. See listings under Series 3.

**Army publications relating to Truck Utility, 1/2 Ton, 4x4, Rover Series 3**

| *Army Code* | *Publication* |
|---|---|
| 22228 | User Hand Book (issued May 1972) |
| 60957 | Servicing Schedule |
| 31361 | Complete Equipment Schedule (24V 90A) |
| 34171 | Complete Equipment Schedule (GS) |
| 34192 | Complete Equipment Schedule (FFR) |
| 61278 | Illustrated Parts Catalogue |

The Series 3 Half-Ton was allocated its own EMER (Wheeled Vehicles) block of Q 020/13 to Q 029/13 and was affected by the general block for all Rovers (SWB and LWB) Q 020 to Q 029. The same blocks covered the CL version. However, confusingly, Trucks Utility, CL 1/2 Ton and 3/4 Ton, 4x4 Rover Series 3 were also allocated block Q 020/18 to Q 029/18.
Also, according to the 1988 index, the following were issued under Q 020/13 to Q 029/13.

**EMER Q 020/13, Data Summary (issued Sept 1975).**
From the main block of EMERs, the following refer to the Half-Ton. Note: If marked all Rover Mks, this indicates all MoD Land Rovers in use on that date were affected, not just the Half-Ton.

**EMER Q 025 Installation Instructions.**

| *Install No.* | *Date of issue* | *Title* |
|---|---|---|
| 15 | Jun 72 | Electrification for internal security duties (all Mks). |
| 19 | Jul 80 | Preparation kit for Radar GS No. 20 Mk 1 Claribel (Half-Ton and 3/4 Ton). |

**EMER Q 025/13 Waterproofing Instructions No. 1, 2, 3 and 4.**

**EMER Q 025/13 Installation Instructions.**

| *Install No.* | *Date of issue* | *Title* |
|---|---|---|
| 5 | May 78 | Culvert mine kit |
| 6 | Aug 81 | GRP protective screening kit. |

**EMER Q 027 Modification Instructions**

| *Mod No* | *Date of issue* | *Title* |
|---|---|---|
| 34 | Mar 73 (No. 2) | Protective screening internal security duties, Rover Mk 6 to II and Half-Ton. |
| 48 | Sep 73 (No. 3) | Modified clutch withdrawal mechanism. |
| 52 | Apr 73 (No. 2) | Fitting of inhibiting device on infra red light. |
| 53 | Oct 72 | Aeon springs for GRP kit, Northern Ireland. |
| 61 | Aug 76 (No. 2) | Installation of line laying kit. Rover 1. |
| 62 | Jun 78 (No. 2) | Modification for aerial cable kit Clansman. |
| 65 | Jun 78 (No. 2) | Modification to accept Clansman radio. |
| 71 | Mar 79 | Load spreader assembly for helicopter transportation. |
| 72 | Dec 79 | New type of battery cover (FFR). |

***Note. Often the date indicates the issue number, i.e. No. 2 = second issue, etc.***
***The Sept 88 EMER index does not list any more modifications after No. 72, so it may be assumed that this was all of them.***

**EMER Q 027/13 Modifications Instructions**

| *Mod No.* | *Date of issue* | *Title* |
|---|---|---|
| 1 | May 78 | Dual brake control for driver training CL models. |
| 2 | Sep 79 | Rack support assembly FFR reinforcement. |
| 3 | Feb 80 | Oil pump moved round 90 degrees. |
| 4 | Dec 79 | Numberplate light fuse (Northern Ireland). |
| 5 | Jun 80 | Discontinue fitting brake vacuum switch. |
| 6 | Jan 81 | Improve gearbox sealing. |

| | | |
|---|---|---|
| 7 | Sep 81 | Radio module, enhanced earth bonding. |
| 8 | May 81 | Battery retention clamps changed (FFR). |
| 9 | Feb 82 | Canvas tilt modified for PRC 344 antenna. |
| 10 | Feb 82 | Bonnet seals to prevent water in air cleaner. |
| 11 | Dec 81 | Modification to carry man pack radios. |
| 12 | Feb 82 | Variable height tow hitch (mainly CL models). |
| 13 | Mar 82 | Fitting headlamp relay to infra red circuit. |

***This is all of them according to the Sept 88 index.***

**EMER Q 029 Miscellaneous instructions**

| *Misc No.* | *Date of issue* | *Title* |
|---|---|---|
| 40 | Apr 78 (No. 3) | Reclipping of oil cooler pipes (all Mks). |
| 41 | Jun 68 | Wheel hubs, grease instead of oil (all Mks). |
| 48 | Feb 72 (No. 2) | Gearbox mainshaft bearing housing (all Mks). |
| 50 | Jul 75 (No. 3) | Redesigned exhaust manifold (all Mks). |
| 58 | Dec 74 | New pattern crankshaft (all Mks). |
| 59 | Jul 75 | Prevention of exhaust manifold cracking (all Mks). |
| 60 | Aug 75 | Rerouting of fuel gauge sense lines (Mk 6 to Rover 1 and early Series 3). |
| 61 | Jul 76 (No 2) | Modification to ammeter shunt box (FFR all Mks). |
| 63 | Oct 76 | Metric engine mounts. |
| 64 | Mar 77 | Nosing attachments for aircraft work (all Mks). |
| 65 | Nov 77 (No. 2) | Lucas D45 distributor without vernier Adjustment. |
| 66 | Oct 78 | Canopy repair technique (all Mks). |

***According to the Sept 88 index Misc. No. 66 was the last issued.***

**EMER Q 029/13 Miscellaneous Instructions**

| *Misc No* | *Date of issue* | *Title* |
|---|---|---|
| 1 | Sept 77 | Fitting of rear seats on CL models. |
| 2 | Feb 78 | Replacement unitary/plugs sockets (FFR). |
| 3 | Apr 78 | Change of brake lining material. |
| 4 | May 78 | New pattern synchronising clutch assembly. |
| 5 | Oct 78 | New pattern head gasket. |
| 6 | Mar 79 | New pattern rotary light switch. |
| 7 | Jul 79 | New pattern cylinder head. |
| 8 | Aug 79 | Distributor Lucas to Ducellier. |
| 9 | Sept 79 | MPH and KPH Speedometers fitted. |
| 10 | Mar 80 | Improvement to front and rear axles. |
| 11 | May 80 | New pattern oil temp transmitter. |
| 12 | Jan 81 | Nomenclature plates missing contract FVE22A/115. |
| 13 | Jan 82 | New pattern safety harness. |

***This is all of them according to the Sept 88 index.***

**Army Equipment Support Publications.**

This system has superseded the earlier EMER publications, and many of the above publications reappeared as AESPs. However, at least one was published which did not appear as an EMER, this was:

2320-D-100-811 Dec 83 Rifle clip support strengthening, vehicles deployed in N. Ireland.
Mod. instr. No. 50.

## Clubs and Restoring a Vehicle

The Half-Ton has always been a very popular vehicle in civilian hands ever since the first Rover 1s were released from service. Many have had a harder life out of the Armed Forces with their civilian owners, as they make excellent off-road machines. Because of this, good original Rover 1s are now rare. Many others have also been re-engined and much modified to their new owners' tastes. If your interest in Lightweights is for off-roading, then any of the local Land Rover clubs should be satisfactory for your needs. However, if you have a particular interest in the marque there exists a number of specialist Land Rover Clubs specifically for the type, these being:

***This early Rover 1 was still a working vehicle at Duxford Airfield with air traffic control in July 2001.***

***The Lightweight is a very popular vehicle in civilian hands. (Courtesy Tom Finlay)***

*Rows of ex-British forces vehicles await new owners at dealers. (Author's Collection)*

*Not all get saved! A Series 3 being broken for spare parts. (Author's Collection)*

**The Lightweight LRC**
Sue Foster
31 Slimbridge Close
Breightmet
Bolton
BL2 5NT
LWLRC@meddle.demon.co.uk
www.meddle.demon.co.uk

**The Ex Military Land Rover Association**
John Butcher
116 Crescent Road
Reading
Berkshire
RG1 5SN

It should be noted that club officials are unpaid volunteers, and are subject to change. The above addresses were correct at the time of publication. A stamped addressed envelope should be enclosed when asking for details of membership, or with a general inquiry, as a matter of courtesy.

The Lightweight LRC caters for all owners of Lightweights, not necessarily just for people keeping vehicles in original condition.

If your aim is to restore a Lightweight to its original military condition and configuration, then you will not go wrong by joining the EMLRA, which is a military vehicle club, but catering for owners of former military Land Rovers. Its members can offer much advice on the military variants of the ma+rque. The club can also provide service histories on recently released British Forces Land Rovers, as well as helping in finding spares and other military paraphernalia. It also produces a newsletter, which gives information on military Land Rovers and related subjects.

Unit service histories for vehicles may be obtained from: (enclose SAE for current prices).

***For Army vehicles:***
The Curator
The Museum of Army Transport
Flemingate
Beverley
North Humberside
HU17 0NG

***For RAF vehicles***
Department of Research & Information Services
The RAF Museum
Grahame Park Way
London
NW9 5LL

# INDEX

9781787115453